BY JOHN HOYLE '57

ILLUSTRATIONS BY JOHN HOYLE, JR. '82

Insite Press
BRYAN, TEXAS

Also by John Hoyle
Good Bull: 30 Years of Aggie Escapades

MANUFACTURED IN THE UNITED STATES OF AMERICA

FIRST EDITION
1 2 3 4 5 6 7 8 9 10

Library of Congress Catalog Number: 90-84888
ISBN: 0-9626069-5-2

*For all the Aggies who
have served in our Armed Forces*

INTRODUCTION

Riding the wave of success from *Good Bull: 30 Years of Aggie Escapades, Bull Number Two* was spawned from the notion of equal rights for Aggie pranksters of the Seventies to the present. The original *Bull* dealt mainly with stories from the Forties, Fifties and Sixties, and the next generations rightly believed they deserved to be heard from as well. Then there were those who didn't care what the time frame, they just wanted to read more. As one Aggie band member said when he called me at home, "The only thing wrong with *Good Bull* is that it isn't long enough."

Letters and calls from Aggies willing to share their tales kept coming, and soon *Bull Two* began to take shape. One tale in particular heralds the changing times, the coming generations, and the notion that as long as there are Aggies, there will be Aggie escapades.

Army Second Lt. Michael Kelly '89 was one of many Aggies who received his copy of *Good Bull* while stationed in the Persian Gulf. A tank platoon leader in the 3rd Infantry Division, Kelly's unit led the 1st Armored Division in engaging and destroying the Republican Guard of Saddam Hussein. Formerly of B-Company in the Fightin' Texas Aggie Band, Kelly wrote to share with me one of his own escapades that took place while he was on training duty in Berlin in 1988. It is to Kelly and all the Aggies who have served and fought in our Armed Forces through the years that we dedicate *Good Bull Number Two*.

THE BERLIN BLITZ . . . Before the historic fall of "The Wall," visitors to Berlin were often stunned by the profusion of graffiti that adorned the grim monument. During training in Berlin, I decided that it was part of my active duty to add a touch of maroon to the decor by emblazing the symbol of Texas A&M on the Berlin Wall.

Braving more than an hour of public transportation, I finally arrived at my destination at the Wall, located in a seedy part of the American Sector, only to have to wait another half-hour while hiding from East German tower guards. Finally, the coast was clear. Removing the can of spray paint with a red top from under my coat — red being the closest color to maroon I could find — I sprayed on the block ATM logo and the phrases "Gig 'em Aggies, BQ '89." I noticed the paint wasn't showing up very well, but chalked it up to the dark night.

Using a flashlight, I re-examined the spray can, only to find out I had purchased clear lacquer. The red cap did not mean red paint. As I trudged back through the bull nettle that surrounds the Wall, and on the long journey back to quarters, I thought to myself, "What an Aggie!"

The next day I returned to the PX, making sure that this time I left with red paint, and braved the bad side of town once again. This time, when I left the Wall, the Aggie monikers were there for all the world to see. I wonder what the German tourists thought when they tried to look up "Gig 'em Aggies" in their English translation books? Call it coincidence, but a little over a year later, the Wall fell.

Michael Kelley
BQ '89

ACKNOWLEDGMENTS

As long as Aggies tell stories about other Aggies, no book of escapades will ever be complete.

Aggies from both the "old school" and from the younger generations urged me to do this sequel, and there are many people to thank for the contents of *Good Bull Two: More Aggie Escapades*. Much credit goes to my family: my wife, Carolyn, for her great listening and editing; my son, John Jr. '82, for the second generation of illustrations; and my daughter-in-law, Julie, whose "traffic control" always got the manuscript where it was supposed to be, on time. A special thanks also to June Wellman who transcribed hours of tales from tape into coherent stories.

The following Aggies and friends of Aggies have contributed stories for *Good Bull Two*: Don Powell '56; Robert Caster Sr. '58; Roy H. Johnson '60; William B. Adair Jr. '73; Robert Murski '73; Polly Patranella; Mike Williams '94; Jackson Reese '94; Greg Reils '94; Dan Debenport '91; John Caster '92; David Wallace '91; Art Deford '92; Jim Jeter '70; John L. Badgett, Ph.D. '68; Phil Pearson '67; Pat Cooper '64; Loyd Taylor '58; Jimmy Williams '55; and Tom Chandler, former Aggie baseball coach.

CONTENTS

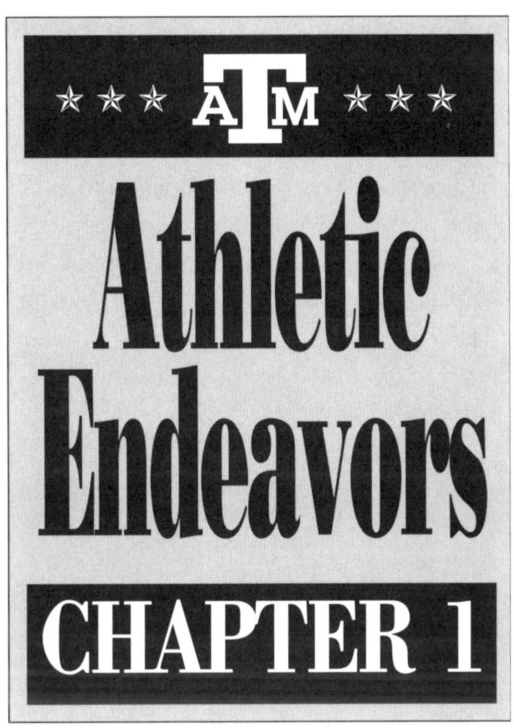

THE REVEILLE BACKFIRE . . .

THE REVEILLE BACKFIRE . . . All Aggies love Reveille, Texas A&M's beautiful Border Collie mascot, cared for so diligently by the Corps of Cadets. It is a great honor to be the student chosen to look after A&M's best friend. Unfortunately, Reveille hasn't always been the most discreet or fastidious creature in the world.

Several years ago, when the Texas A&M football stadium was real grass, Reveille would stand patiently on the sidelines while the great Fightin' Texas Aggie Band performed in front of thousands. Just as the band would finish, Reveille would sprint to the center of the field and do her number on the 50 yard line. Naturally, the crowd would go bananas.

As it happened, Reveille chose to grace the field during a big ball game against Baylor. Sure enough, the band did their wonderful performance and then Reveille did hers, right on the 50 yard line. After halftime, A&M kicked off to Baylor and Baylor made a couple of good gains up to the 49 yard line. On first down for Baylor, a great All-American tailback grabbed the football and had just started off when Charlie, Texas A&M's great All-American tackle, nailed him. You could hear the impact all over the stadium; no gain.

The Aggies lined up in their defensive huddle and Lloyd, the defensive captain, started to call the signals when he suddenly stopped and said, "What's that smell? It's awful!" He looked accusingly at Charlie and said, "What is that?" Charlie held up both arms, revealing the remnants of Reveille's surprise package.

If Reveille could talk, no doubt she would have said, "Sorry, Charlie. I left that for Baylor, not for you."

SMOKEY AND THE WHIRLPOOL . . . During the Bear

Bryant years, Texas A&M had a football head trainer called Smokey. Smokey was legendary, not only because he was hard of hearing, but because he was hard on anyone or anything that didn't measure up to his somewhat quaint standards. He was especially vocal about the administration whenever they chopped another tree down on campus or created another rule that Smokey adjudged to be superfluous.

He would wander around complaining to all within earshot, "The only thing around here worth a damn, and they cut the damn things down."

The student athletes just loved him. The only problem was, whenever anyone was injured, Smokey invoked the same universal cure-all — the whirlpool.

"Anything you got hurt, put it in the whirlpool for at least five minutes," he would intone. "If it still hurts, put it in there for another five minutes."

Well, usually the hot circulating water would help an injury, but every once in a while there would come along an exception to his universal rule. Ty, a student from Brenham, Texas, wasn't any Nobel Prize winner, and there were even those who said he was about three ice cubes short of a tray. Smokey walked in one day to find the huge lineman with his head down in that hot swirling water. It so scared Smokey that he grasped the guy by the hair, yanking him out of the whirlpool. Ty was spitting and sputtering as Smokey demanded, "What are you doing, you crazy fool?"

The dazed lineman looked at him, saying, "Well, Smokey, I had a terrible headache and you said five minutes in the whirlpool would cure anything. I had already gone for two minutes, but I don't think I was going to make five. Thanks for pulling me out."

As it turned out, Smokey saved a star. Ty went on to Hollywood and found fame as a cowboy actor.

HOG WILD . . . Athletic trainers and managers have always been

respected for the job they do in organizing equipment, taking care of players' injuries, and all other details that are so important and vital to a successful athletic program, but they also play a big roll in motivating the team to win. On the eve of a big game against Arkansas, a well-known figure in athletic training decided that the Aggies were sorely lacking in the enthusiasm that would be required to skin the Hogs.

After some thoughtful debate, "Willie" decided on a plan and informed the coach and other trainers. Sure enough, that afternoon, during the final practice before the big game, the players were halfheartedly walking through the drills. No amount of yelling and screaming from the coaches could get the players fired up. "Willie" decided to act.

It was a raw, wet day, no more than 41 degrees, and the players were dragging listlessly around the field. All of a sudden, from underneath Kyle Field comes the wildest looking figure you have ever seen. Stripped to the motivating essentials, here comes this well-respected trainer clad only in a jock strap and an Arkansas Razorback Hog hat screaming like a banshee, "Sooey pig, Sooey pig, Soooeey pig."

Up and down the field he ran, hollering and yelling. The football team went berserk as the hog hat-wearing maniac disappeared back underneath the stands. The team completed their practice with a never-before-seen spirit and

motivation. That Saturday, the Aggies overwhelmed the Hogs 30-6.

From that day on, a hog hat and a jock strap were added to the athletic training staff's bag of essentials.

12ᵀᴴ MAN AND THE HEISMAN TOWEL...

The Texas Aggie football team became Southwest Conference Champions in the season of 1987 and met the great Notre Dame team in the 1988 Cotton Bowl. It was a terrific game which we all know the Aggies won, but one play in the game also gave birth to an instant tradition and thousands of dollars in souvenir revenues.

Notre Dame had a Heisman Trophy-winning halfback receiver that the

Aggies knew they had to stop. Early in the ballgame, the 12th Man Team, which was started by Coach Jackie Sherrill, lined up for a kickoff. This 12th Man team had some lunatics on it who had no concern for their bodies. They believed they embodied all the power of the nearly 40,000-member Texas A&M student body, and they were determined to get a piece of the opposing team even if it meant putting themselves in harm's way.

The kickoff went to the goal line and it was received by the great Notre Dame player. He started up the field and was quickly crunched by one of the 12th Man squad members out on a suicide mission. The lad blasted the All-American, knocking him down, and the play stopped. The next thing the fans saw was the All-American running across the field, tackling the 12th Man guy. Nobody was sure what was happening; they thought the All-American had lost his mind. After the tackle, the Notre Dame player retrieved the towel that the 12th Man player had snagged as a souvenir.

At the start of the next season, thousands of Aggie fans could be seen waving 12th Man spirit towels in the stands. The 12th Man player never made All-American and never started on the regular team, but he will go down in history as the guy who put the lick on the Heisman trophy winner and started a tradition in the process. Gig'em Aggies.

Hot Dog Football Photographer . . .

Back when Kyle Field was a little bit smaller and an all-grass surface, a traveling photographer was making the rounds of all the major universities, taking pictures of football players and putting them on life-size posters. Being a business man, the photographer would then sell these posters to the football players at a pretty good price.

The photographer was the hot-dog type with a peculiar sort of personality. The day he came driving up in his big pink Cadillac to Kyle Field stadium, he pulled up and parked right on the football field. Without so much as a "How do you do," he lined up about nine of those life-size posters right behind the Cadillac. He then proceeded to bring the players around and hawk his posters.

Before long, he had set up all his photography equipment and was busy taking pictures, mentally tallying up the dollars he would make off the Aggies.

About that time, the football trainer came driving by on a tractor. Trying to do his job maintaining the field was impossible with the pink Cadillac parked in the way.

"Hey, you, get that car out of my way!" he admonished the photographer.

"You get it out of the way," came the insolent reply. "I'm busy here, taking pictures of these great football players."

The trainer jumped off the tractor and stalked over to the photographer. Flipping his keys at the trainer, the photographer yelled, "You drive the thing."

The trainer got in the pink Cadillac and fired it up. He popped it into "R," figuring that stood for "race," and backed over every one of those nine life-size posters. He mowed them down like they were the grass on the field.

The players just fell apart laughing. As the trainer jumped out of the Cadillac and threw the keys back to the photographer, he said, "Sorry about that. I didn't know anything was behind me."

With that, he jumped back on his tractor and went about his way. Whether another football player ever received a life-size poster after that day is not known.

TANK, THE INTIMIDATER . . . Basketball at Texas A&M

University has seen some championship days and some other kinds of days, as well. Of all the players that have come and gone, many will remember one athlete who made a unique contribution to his team.

"Big John, the Tank," had been a fine high school basketball player in Oklahoma and was recruited by Coach John Floyd to help the sagging fortunes of the Aggie team. As a high school player, Big John weighed in at about 195 pounds and was 6'2" tall. After he came to campus and got acquainted with the chow at Sbisa Dining Hall, Big John ballooned up to 260 pounds. There went his basketball quickness and power, but he was on scholarship so he stayed on the team. During his sophomore year, Big John spent a lot of time on the bench, but Coach Floyd knew just when and how to use his special talents.

During a game against SMU, the Aggies were taking a beating at the hands of SMU's All-American center. He was really scoring a lot of points and snagging all the rebounds. Floyd says, "John, go in there and do what you need to do."

The crowd starts yelling, "Big John, Big John, Big John... Tank, Tank, Tank," as he entered the game. The first thing Big John did was grab the All-American center by the pants and pulled them half down. He then grabbed the fellow's arm, jerked him around and poked him in the ribs. This made the All-American so mad that he turned around and took a swing at Big John.

Big John ducked and turned to the referee imploring, "He is trying to kill me, ref." The ref threw the All-American out of the ballgame. Shortly thereafter, Coach Floyd quietly removed Big John from the game and the Aggies went on to victory.

That play made Big John famous to more than just the home crowd. In another game, Big John got to play against Tulane over in New Orleans. Because a player was hurt, he got more court time than usual. After the game, as the Aggies were boarding the train home, a porter said, "I saw that basketball game tonight. Where is Tank?"

"Right here, sir," Tank replied.

"Son, how could anybody get four fouls in just two minutes?" the porter asked.

"It's easy," came Big John's reply.

Years later, Big John, the Tank, went on to become a successful business leader, shedding both his weight and his nickname.

LITTLE TEX AND THE "BEAR" . . . Texas A&M has

always had its legendary athletes: King Gill, John Kimbrough, John David Crow, Jack Pardee, Randy Matson, Bubba Bean, John Byington, Lori Stoll, Linda Walton, Darren Lewis and many, many others. However, sometimes an unknown athlete will rise to the occasion and do spectacular things to help the Aggies win a big one.

In 1955, when Texas A&M was battling for the Southwest Conference baseball championship, one of the batting practice pitchers was named Tex Vanzura from Austin. Little Tex was about 5'10" and 150 pounds soaking wet. He had been a good high school pitcher, but was not good enough to pitch regularly on that championship staff. However, he did contribute a lot to batting practice and team spirit.

The championship game came down to the last game of the season against the SMU Mustangs in Dallas. This was a "must win" situation to give Texas A&M its first undisputed baseball championship in 20 years. A&M and SMU both started their aces. There was a crowd of four to five thousand there at Armstrong Field, and the game was started late because it had been raining. The Aggies went ahead in the ninth inning with a base hit by John Stockton, the centerfielder. In the bottom of the ninth inning, one of the regular pitchers of the Aggie staff faltered and loaded the bases. Coach Bell called on, who else, Tex.

Bear Bryant, the legendary football coach, was in the stands watching this game; he loved baseball. Little Tex took the mound. The rest of the players were puzzled as to why the coach would bring in a batting practice pitcher. But the coach knew that this little man had a big heart and was a great competitor.

SMU was able to peck out only one run to tie the ball game. The Aggies came back in the top of the 10th, and went one run ahead. Tex came back in the bottom of the 10th inning. He struck out two, and got the final out on a ground ball to third base. The Championship belonged to the Aggies.

The first one on the field was Bear Bryant. He grabbed Tex, put him on his

shoulders and walked him around saying, "When it comes to guts, this little man ought to get the Oscar."

Tex was a true hero on that day and will always be remembered by the members of that championship team.

👍

WET FROGS AND WET WOMEN . . . Back before women students were allowed at Texas A&M University, the fairer sex would come in on buses and trains from Texas Women's University and towns all over Texas for big football weekends. In the mid-Fifties, the Texas Aggies had their great teams with Jack Pardee, Dennis Goehring, Lloyd Taylor and John David Crow playing for Coach Bear Bryant.

There was a big game scheduled against TCU with its great running back, Jim Swink. Rain started to fall during the tight ballgame that would decide the championship. Suddenly, a tornado hit College Station, coming dangerously close to Kyle Field. The skies blackened and torrential rains came down. Texas A&M was leading 7-6 and TCU was on the one foot line.

Fans couldn't see the goal line, or anything else, for the mud and the rain. Swink hit the line and the TCU team starts yelling, "We've scored." But the official said no. Swink was given the ball again and boom — he hit the line and again TCU thought they had scored. Again, the officials denied.

The third time, the Aggie defense stiffened, Swink took the ball off tackle and A&M stopped him, obviously shy of the goal line. One of the Aggie defenders was heard to say, "What's the matter, All-American, can't you score?"

To this day, TCU officials, coaches, and players still think they scored. The Aggies and the record book will tell you that they didn't.

During that wet and feverish ballgame, the students and their transported dates got so wet and cold they conceived a desperate measure. Two Aggies and their dates ran back to the dorm where the dates dried off and put on borrowed sets of fatigues and army field jackets. They returned to the field in time to see the rest of the football game.

Long before there were other females on campus, on that day, there were two women who were unofficially the first members of the Corps of Cadets.

THE T.U. SWEEP . . . "Aggies Sweep the Longhorns 4-1, 8-4 and 7-6." These headlines shocked the college baseball world in the spring of '91; few people had expected the Aggies to win even one game, much less three games against the nation's third-ranked Longhorns.

Dreams of a sweep were dancing in the Aggies' heads after the opening game win, and fans returned for the second game with brooms in hand.

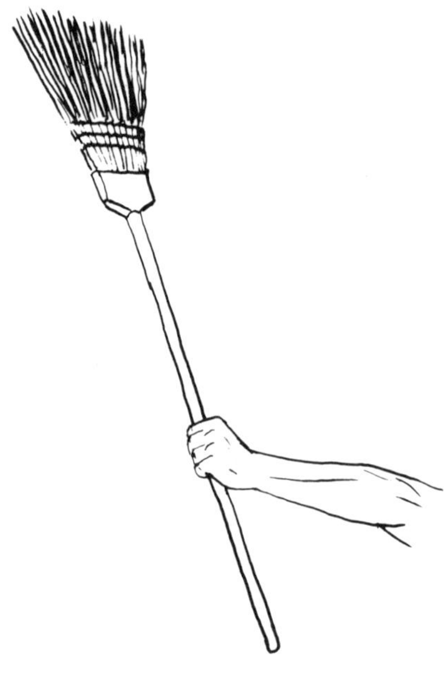

Unfortunately, officials at the gate de-broomed everyone, fearing the spirit sticks might prove hazardous in the heat of competition. A&M won the second game after a bench-clearing base brawl in the fifth inning, and a disgruntled t.u. pitcher made an obscene gesture to the Aggie fans along the first base line as he trudged off the field.

His gesture brought out the brooms. Somehow, several enterprising fans had managed to sweep by the officials at the gate. It took a come-from-behind effort in the final game to complete the sweep and, after the game, jubilant Aggie fans mobbed the field, brooms held high, joining the players in a raucous rendition of the Aggie War Hymn.

The Aggies had managed to go from last to first place in the conference standings. In a sweeping statement, Coach Johnson said, "This was just our weekend."

*DON'T MESS AROUND WITH JIM . . .*The great 1989 baseball team had been number one for eleven weeks in a row when they faced off against the Arkansas Razorbacks. Tensions were high as the winner would walk away with the Southwest Conference Baseball championship title.

Two runs down in the bottom of the ninth, worried Aggies saw a glimmer of hope as Big Jim stepped up to bat with two men on. The umpire called a strike, but Big Jim didn't looked fazed. When the next pitch was called a strike, Jim, along with several thousand Aggie fans, thought the umpire ought to re-think his call. Jim and the umpire faced off, jawing about the call while the fans went wild in the stands. It seemed as though only seconds remained before Jim and the Aggies' hopes of a win would be thrown out of the park.

Running from the dugout, the Aggie coach threw himself between Jim and the umpire. Gesturing at the out-of-control crowd, the coach managed to turn the umpire's attention away from Jim. When a near state of calm had returned to the park, Jim once again stepped up to bat.

A self-satisfied smirk on the face of the Hog pitcher said that he knew Jim was so rattled by his near ejection, the third strike, and the game, was in the bag. He wound up and let it fly.

Big Jim pounded the ball over the head of the left fielder and off the wall, bringing in the two Aggies on base and tying the score. The play got the Aggies back in the game and a hit by Blake Pyle broke the Hogs' back, giving the Aggies the game and the championship title.

As the song says, you don't mess around with Jim. Jim Neuman, that is.

BOMBING THE REFS . . . Aggie basketball fans have never

been too fond of referees, especially those that need a lot of horse laughs during a ballgame. On one occasion, the home crowd definitely felt it had been the referees who had beaten the Aggies instead of the other team.

After the game, the unpopular refs slithered off the court to the upstair's dressing room to change. Two Aggies in particular couldn't let the defeat go. Still hot about the calls, they decided to retaliate with an athletic skill of their own — heaving water bombs made out of big nickel balloons.

Slipping around behind G. Rollie White Coliseum, the two Aggies spotted the referees, fully dressed in sport coats and ties. With a reputation for remarkable accuracy with water bombs from about 35 yards, these two Aggies had perfected a way of heaving them, much like a discus thrower.

Clyde was first; he spun around and let fly. The water balloon flattened out like the top of a trash can, sailing right through the second-floor window, catching both referees as they sat in folding chairs. All that could be heard after the assault were a few curse words, a little screaming and the sounds of two Aggies sprinting off into the night.

The assault squad scored a definite foul, but the Aggies felt like it was the only fair call of the night.

A LEGEND BEATS LSU . . . Although it was not an official

Corps Trip, many cadets banded together and headed for the big LSU rivalry in the fall of 1970. Some 2,000 loyal Aggies were seated in the end zone of the "Tiger-Pit" that night, enduring the empty liquor bottles thrown by LSU fans that cascaded down on their heads.

The crowd was wild, and the highly ranked LSU team and 66,000 screaming, boozed Cajuns did not approve of Aggies in any form or fashion.

With thirteen seconds to go, the Ags were behind and deep in their own territory when the quarterback let go with a long pass down the middle of the field. The lone receiver was headed in the direction of the faithful 2,000 good

Ags in the far end zone. The ball floated down into his hands and the two pursuing Tigers hadn't a prayer of catching him.

When Hugh McElroy scored the winning touchdown that night, he became the first of many black Aggie football legends to come, and only the second black player in the team's history.

After the Aggies scored, the enraged Cajuns mobbed the fans and field, and the loyal Aggies never got to see the extra point or LSU's final play as the clock ran out.

THE SBISA VOLUNTEER & HOT LUBE . . .

For many years, students worked their way through college at Texas A&M by waiting tables at the Sbisa and Duncan chow halls. Called Sbisa and Duncan volunteers, these dedicated young men got up at 5:30 a.m., ran to the chow halls, put on their white jackets, got their serving trays, set the tables and awaited the onrush of hungry cadets.

Each Sbisa volunteer was responsible for three tables of about thirty Aggies, so it took a lot of hard work and energy to run back and forth between the tables and the kitchen. Most of the time, the student body was courteous to these hard-working volunteers, but every once in a while, somebody would press his luck by taunting the workers.

One day, a senior kept bitching and moaning about the quality of service, yelling, "More bullneck, more spud, more shot. Hurry up, freshman, what's taking you so long?

"Bring us more hot lube, more spuds, more gunwadding. Why didn't we get more cush when we got more cow!"

The poor, frustrated freshman was already operating at a dead run to keep the cadets supplied with hot gravy and potatoes, and the senior's criticism didn't go down too well.

Running back to the kitchen, he loaded up a big bowl of hot gravy on his tray and headed for the senior, yelling, "Hot stuff, hot stuff, hot stuff, out of my way!" He came to a sliding stop, but the gravy continued on its intended course, right down the backside of the loudmouthed senior.

The senior jumped up yelling and screaming, while his tablemates could hardly refrain from laughing.

"Do you have any excuse, freshman?" demanded the scalded senior.

"Yes sir," came the reply. "I yelled hot stuff and I guess you just didn't move fast enough."

The senior decided that the situation called for discretion and wisely refrained from further abuse of the freshman for fear of where he might be served next time.

*S*WATTING *S*ERGEBUTTS . . . Years ago, it was customary for freshman cadets to receive punishment at the hands of paddle-wielding upperclassmen.

Fish questioned the wisdom of this "tradition" then and, fortunately, they need not worry about it today. Nonetheless, it was once part of the lore that is Texas A&M.

After an offense was committed, an upperclassman would apply the appropriate number of swats to the bottom of the erring freshman. Of course, the appropriate number was determined by the upperclassman. Sometimes, it seemed as though the swats were administered for no other crime than just being a poor freshman.

One year, the freshman band members got together and vowed that they would not submit to the discipline of the board. Together, they were determined to break the cycle of "swats." The class ahead of them became frustrated with the pact, but the Fish prevailed and ended the year without a swat among them. Even after the group returned to campus the following year as sophomores, their unforgiving classmates, now juniors, still seethed with frustration over the No Swats Pack.

That year, the band traveled to Lubbock for a football game against the Texas Tech Red Raiders. The band was quartered in a series of old huts on the Tech campus with each class taking a separate building. During the night, the juniors, known as Sergebutts in Corps lingo, entered the No Swats Pack's building, determined to end the non-Aggie pact. It was the logic of the Sergebutts that even though they were now sophomores, or Pissheads, the pack would always be considered Fish until they submitted to the board.

The Pissheads pretended to be asleep, which took a lot of imagination since the Sergebutts were banging the ends of their metal cots with the boards. But still they would not move. Finally, in a frenzy of frustration, the Sergebutts retreated to their hut.

A short while later, the sophomores were amazed by strange sounds emanating from the juniors' hut. It seems that the Sergebutts' long frustration had finally peeked and they had started beating each other!

After that night, the two classes never mentioned the board again, and within a few years, hazing with a board disappeared. Incoming freshmen at Texas A&M can thank the "No Swats Pack" for the part they played in ending this questionable tradition at Texas A&M.

*T*HE *S*OLE OF AN *A*GGIE . . . The day you were issued your military uniforms at Texas A&M set the style, so to speak, for the rest of your year. Those issuing uniforms generally did their best to make sure you were properly covered, but expediency was more highly valued than whatever fashion statement your uniform might make. Often they would hand you an article of clothing, saying simply, "Next."

"But sir, this doesn't fit."

"Next!"

Your uniform package included khaki pants and shirts, macho helmet liners, helmets and those unforgettably attractive black army-issue shoes. The shoes always came with a stern warning to "Bring these back just the way you got them." Generations of Aggies never understood that admonition — how could you wear something every day for one full year and bring it back just the way you found it?

And so it was that one poor Aggie from Comanche ran amok of the shoe rule. Like most Aggies of his era, this poor soul didn't have much money, and he literally wore out his pair of shoes; the holes were about the size of a fifty-cent piece. At the end of the semester, upon re-reading his instructions to "Bring them back like new," he did what any good Aggie would do when confronted by the dual problems of holes in the soles and no money to get them repaired.

Applying a little Aggie engineering to the dilemma, he took his last nickel and purchased some bubble gum. Now this bubble gum, chewed awhile and then mixed with brown dirt, made an excellent camouflage for those holes in both shoes. He turned them in, passed inspection and went on about his way.

Creativity is the mother of invention, and it would be instructive to learn what the next unfortunate Aggie who walked a mile in those shoes had to do to save his soles.

THE DISAPPEARING FRESHMAN . . . One of the traditions at Texas A&M is that all Fish in the Corps must "whip out" to Pissheads, Sergebutts, and seniors, remembering their names and where they are from. Just seeing an upperclassman is enough to strike fear in the heart of a Fish. They can think of nothing else except running up, whipping out, introducing themselves and remembering the seniors', juniors', or sophomores' names in order to stay out of trouble.

A Fish who hailed from Texline, Texas, was determined to impress his superiors. Early in the year he had learned all the names of the guys in his outfit; he was an Aggie's Aggie. Over close to Rudder Theater, along where Military Walk used to be, a senior was passing within sight of the gung-ho Fish. Hurrying to make a good impression, the Fish tucked his books under his left arm and headed at a dead run over to the senior.

Just as he whipped out and grabbed the senior's hand, the single-minded Fish stepped where a manhole cover had been left off the entrance to a steam tunnel. The poor fish disappeared from sight, books spinning through the air. Fortunately, the senior had a good grip on the freshman and was able to hold onto to the dangling Fish.

There was the senior, down on his knees, trying to land a 160-pound Fish from a manhole. A couple of other Aggies ran over and helped retrieve the fallen freshman. The first words out of his mouth as he emerged from the hole were, "Glad to meet you, sir, where are you from, sir?"

He never missed a lick. In the future, however, he did develop "tunnel vision" to go along with his relentless pursuit of duty.

PISSHEAD PRIVILEGE . . . One of the more recent Corps traditions allows freshmen to take on Pisshead privileges on a certain day during the school year. For instance, if you are a Fish member of the Class of '93, on the 93rd day of the school year, you become a Pisshead for one day. In a particular Air Force outfit, one Pisshead had been giving the freshmen big-time hell all through the school year, making them run his errands and clean his room. He had these poor little Fish setting records for new heights every time he said "jump." However, as tradition dictated, on the 93rd day they became Pissheads and revenge was at hand.

These freshmen were innovative. It seems that their tormentor looked somewhat like a hairy ape; he had hair all over his body. So the inspired Pissheads-for-a-day paid a visit to the athletic trainer's office and acquired some supplies before heading back to Dorm 9.

There they found the ape man sitting on the steps reading a Houston newspaper.

"Howdy," intoned the Fish.

The Pisshead looked a little surprised and said, "Howdy, hell . . . Howdy, WHO, Fish?"

"Not today, we're not!" they exclaimed as the five of them jumped him, dragged him into his room, stripped him down and set to work. It took two rolls of athletic tape to completely tape him to his bed post. He looked like a mummy. The merry band of tapers made a hasty departure, leaving the Pisshead in his unfortunate predicament.

Hours went by before one of the Pisshead's buddies finally heard his muffled bleating. Of course, the whole outfit was invited into the room to see the spectacle, and only after a good time was had by all, at the "mummy's" expense, did they start the delicate task of trying to remove the tape from that hairy body.

There are some who will tell you that, as much as three weeks later, the sophomore was still walking around with tape hanging off his back. But he did become very good friends with the freshmen . . . lest they decide to play tapes on him again.

ALL FOR ONE, IN LOVE AND WAR . . . One

weekend, a Pisshead was sitting despondent, his face in his hands. Two Fish passed by and enquired, "Sir, what's wrong?"

"I got a 'Dear John' letter," came the remorseful reply. "My sweetheart back home is dating some other guy."

The two Fish could see how upset the poor fellow was over the flush letter, and it was still on their minds about two weeks later when they went home to Jacksboro for the weekend. Heading out to Jack's Night Club, who should Fate send their way but the Pisshead's ex-girlfriend, busy dancing and having a good time with another fellow.

Now, Aggies take all relationships seriously, and an insult to one is an insult to all, so the two Fish marched right over to the recently departed girlfriend and said, "You did our buddy wrong, and we want you to apologize to him. Besides that, what are you doing hanging around with this turkey?"

That didn't go over too well with the "turkey" who just happened to be a teasipper; a fight ensued. The owner broke up the ruckus and threw them all out of the place. Before leaving, the Aggies let the young woman know how unhappy they were about the way she had treated their good friend and told her how unfair she was.

She cried a little, thought it over, went to the phone and called her Aggie, saying, "You must really love me to have two freshman come and beat up on my date."

He said, "I do," and eventually she did, too — they got back together, were married two years later and lived happily ever after.

BEAR CRAWL TO THE BRAZOS . . . Senior cadets

normally are mature, follow the rules, and try to set a good example for their underclassmen. However, every once in a while, even seniors get a little wild in the midst of a celebration.

A group of seniors, returning from a Corps trip late one Sunday night, was feeling no pain and decided to raise a little hell in the dorm.

There was a certain Pisshead who thought he was "holier than thou" and took a dislike to the seniors' ruckus. Rather than going out and telling them to knock it off, he called the local police and reported a disturbance in Dorm 4. The police answered the call with sirens screaming and lights flashing. They went to the dorm and nabbed the seniors.

"What is this all about?" demanded the seniors.

"Well, you have been reported as creating a nuisance," replied the police.

When the seniors demanded to know the source of the complaint, the police refused, saying, "We don't have to say who told us anything."

But the Corps is no place to try and keep a secret and before long, word got back to the seniors that it had been Pisshead Jones who had sicced the police on them.

The following day, the Corps staff required the seniors to fill out a multitude of reports and to be in the commandant's office at 8 a.m. sharp to respond to the charges against them. After two weeks of trials and tribulations, the seniors were faced with disciplinary action. They accepted the discipline like good Aggies and later graduated.

It is also part of the legend that the Pisshead who ratted on them did a bear crawl from Dorm 4 to the Brazos River Bridge, five miles away, and back. That was the last time he reported any senior for making too much noise on a Sunday night.

THE FISH WITH TWO LEFT FEET . . . Military outfits at Texas A&M take a lot of pride in their marching skills, each year competing for the coveted Simpson Drill Award. Outfit C-2 had won the Simpson Award two years in a row, and they were confident they were headed for a third victory until the C.O. discovered he had one Fish who didn't know his left foot from his right one.

The creative commander ordered the freshman to always carry a rock in his left hand when marching to remind him which foot was which.

The day of the big competition arrived, and the C.O. made sure the cadet had brought along his rock. Company C-2 proudly stepped off, with the Fish hidden safely in the middle of the ranks. They put on a tremendous show. Finally, just as they marched past the Review Stand, the commander barked, "Left flank!" Sure enough, everybody went left flank except the one lone Fish who went right, knocking one of his buddies down. The Commander then yelled, "Right flank," and the entire outfit turned right except for the dazed Fish who had yet to figure out what was wrong. Again he turned the wrong way, felling another Aggie in his wayward path. His buddies dragged him back into the ranks, picked up their fallen comrades and marched off to a last place finish in the contest.

The commander grabbed the backward freshman, yelling, "I thought you were carrying a rock with you! Let me see it." The freshman extended his right hand and there was the rock.

The commander hadn't taken into account that if the Aggie didn't know his left foot from his right foot, there was a better than average chance that he wouldn't know his left hand from his right hand either.

THE COMMANDANTS MISSING BUG . . . Back

in the Seventies, the Corps commandant drove a little yellow Volkswagen bug around campus. It was an older model and had a few rattles, but he was really proud of it. He always parked it out in front of the Corps area next to Dorm 4.

There was a Fish in the Corps whose dad had been a classmate of the commandant's back in the Fifties. It seems that the commandant had once played a trick on this freshman's dad by hiding his car for two weeks. 'Lo these many years later, the dad still had revenge on his mind and decided to enlist the help of his son. Together the pair plotted their coup.

Upon leaving his office one night, the Commandant's beloved bug was nowhere to be found. He asked around but nobody knew its whereabouts. The police did not know either. Stolen car alerts were issued, but not until some three weeks later did a rumor reach the commandant's office that his Volkswagen was on the roof of Dorm 4.

Sure enough, there it perched, in all its yellow glory. The commandant, the police and nearly everyone else were at a loss to explain the car's reappearance in such a strange location. Everyone except the Fish, a few of his buddies, and, of course, his dad.

It seems that after the commandant parked his car that morning, the Fish and his buddies hot wired it and drove it to the outskirts of College Station. Taking it apart, they returned the car to campus in the back of three pick-ups. By the end of the day, the Volkswagen had been carried piece by piece in duffel bags to the roof of Dorm 4. Over the next three weeks, the car had been completely reassembled on the roof.

When the commandant first located his car, he was understandably upset. The buddies never ratted on each other and, with no one to blame, the commandant decided to see the humor in the situation and leave the VW in its new parking spot. He bought himself a used pickup.

At the end of the year, the Outfit in Dorm 4 disassembled the Volkswagen again, carried it down, and put it together once again, only this time at ground level. They then delivered it to the front of the commandant's house.

Whether or not the father-son duo ever confessed is unclear, but it goes to show that no matter how many years go by, revenge is still sweet.

THE MOTHER OF ALL WATER FIGHTS . . .

Perhaps the biggest water fight in all of A&M's history occurred a few years ago between the band and some jocks from an armored division. There had been several grudge battles leading up to the grand event, and the feud was well established.

The problem was, the cadets (known as CTs) would organize several outfits until they outnumbered the band (called BQs) and then do them in. The CTs felt they were far superior to the BQs on the battle field of water fights and believed themselves to be invincible. Little did they know.

The band designed a grand plan to incite a water fight with the jock outfit in Dorm 12. Late one evening, after the Corps of Supervisors had retired for the night, half of the band members lined up in front of Dorm 12 and started playing the t.u. fight song. The jocks were enraged. They threw on fatigues, manned their water buckets and prepared to charge. They launched the attack on the BQs while they were still in formation playing the offensive song.

Just as the jocks charged out of the dorm to attack, the other half of the BQs charged from an ambush position behind the playing members, dousing the jocks with water before the entire band turned to run. As predicted, the jocks followed in hot pursuit toward the band dorm.

Just as the BQs reached the safety of their dorm, yet another group of enterprising BQs came around the corner of the quad in a huge red fire truck with four hoses pumping water at high velocity. A CT named Bob was one of the first jocks to round the corner, and a stream of water hit him with such force it knocked the buttons off of his fatigues, almost ripping his clothes completely off. He was knocked about four feet backwards and watched as all his jock

buddies scattered like bowling pins across the concrete yard in front of the band dorm.

Glasses and clothes were flying amid the jock's yells and screams as the hoses kept pumping, blasting everybody that tried to get up. Huge flood lights on the fire truck blinded the jocks and, with the sirens wailing and the water blasting, it was a sight to behold. Finally, one of the CTs wisely yelled, "Retreat! Retreat!" The jocks crawled back to their dorm with the unrelenting BQs still in hot pursuit.

The fire truck, which had been secreted in from South Texas, was eventually returned, but not until after it had been used to turn the tide in the Mother of All Water Fights.

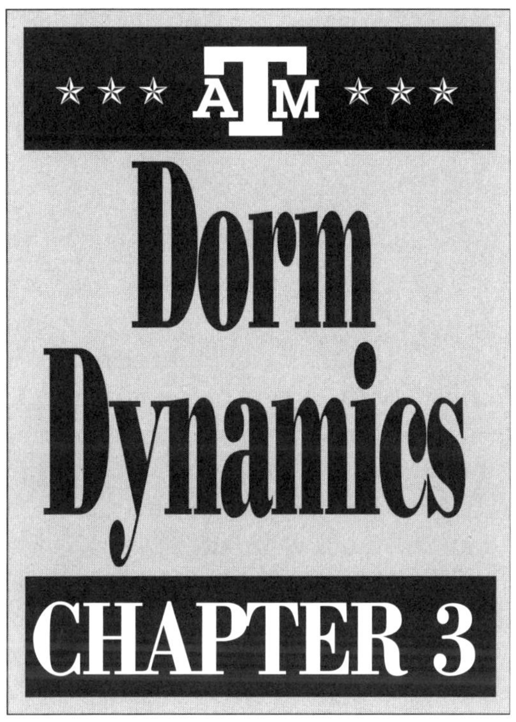

FISH GUILT TRIP . . . One of the no-no's in the Corps is to have a member of the opposite sex in your dorm room at the wrong hours. One night, a group of Fish saw a senior sneaking a young woman into his room. The freshmen, who were jealous anyway, decided fast action and quick thinking were needed to save the senior from himself.

Gathering outside the senior's room, one of the group said, "Let's serenade him. Everybody, now, all together — "Jesus Loves Me."

Inside the room, the senior and his girl were castigated by the piety of this fine old religious hymn, hearing "Jesus loves me this I know, for the Bible tells me so..."

The next thing you know, lights were visible under the door and soon the senior and his girl emerged with sheepish looks on their faces.

The freshmen had won again.

👍

THE *R.A.'s RINSE* . . . Resident Advisors in the dormitories at Texas A&M University are dedicated, hard working professionals who are also students. Among their many responsibilities are keeping the dorms quiet and making sure that the students follow the rules. Sometimes, however, the rules, and the R.A.'s, get on the students' nerves.

Two students, Jean and Carol, were out in the hall in Mosher Dormitory. Unaware that an R.A. was watching, Carol launched a well-aimed water balloon at Jean, blasting her on the back of the head. Water went everywhere. The outraged R.A. yelled and screamed and made them mop up the mess. Then, without waiting to cool off, the R.A. reported the pranksters to University authorities instead of handling the discipline herself. Jean and Carol were officially reprimanded. Though the action caused no permanent harm, the students felt betrayed. They decided to get revenge.

Going over to Northgate, Jean, Carol and a half dozen commiserating pals purchased a package of 150 balloons and spent all weekend filling them with water. The over-zealous R.A. was gone that weekend, leaving the avengers free to carefully and gingerly stack the 150 water balloons to about 6 to 7 feet high in the center of the R.A.'s room.

Sunday evening came, and the balloon squad appeared nonchalant as they greeted the returning R.A. Watching her disappear inside her room, the group was almost instantly rewarded with a loud, gargling scream. It seems that the R.A. had tried to pick up two of the balloons, dropped them by mistake, setting off a contagion of wet distress. It took two days to dry out the room and get it cleaned up.

The R.A. was upset, but wisely decided not to conduct an investigation into the balloon bomb-out, figuring it was a worthwhile, albeit wet, lesson in leadership.

THE PLAYFUL PYTHON . . . A few years ago, a young

woman from Vidor, in southeast Texas, brought her pet along to enroll at Texas A&M. She loved her pet and talked about how cute it was; never mind that the pet happened to be a five-foot baby python. As it happened, the young lady did not have a roommate for the first three or four weeks of school while the University attempted to organize all the new room assignments.

When the news finally arrived that a roommate would be forthcoming, she had only minutes to decide what to do with her python until a more relaxed and leisurely introduction could be arranged. His cage being out in the car, she quickly popped the pet into a nearby laundry bag, just as the new roommate came down the hall. Quickly, she stowed the bagged booty in the closet before turning to greet her new roommate who arrived loaded down with clothes and other bundles.

The new roommate was eager to put her things away and settle in but, fearful she would find the python prematurely, the pet-owner said, "Okay, but I'm sorry, I seem to have the closet completely full. Just put your things here along the wall, and I will clean the closet out later."

Still unsure how to introduce the room's third occupant, the python owner went down the hall to get a Coke and to ponder the snakey business. Determined to get settled, the new roommate decided to help out by getting started with the closet cleaning. Digging around, she found the laundry bag and decided to consolidate space by adding her own dirty clothes to the bag.

Screams that could be heard across campus announced that the new roommate and the python had engaged in unplanned introductions. Racing back to her room, the pet owner found her hysterical roommate dashing around the room with a somewhat bewildered python hanging onto her arm.

Though all recovered and eventually made peace with one another, you can be assured that was the last time the roommate ever reached into anybody's laundry bag.

♦

THE BOOBY-TRAPPED HIGHJUMP . . . Aggies

have strange ways of playing practical jokes on each other. In the Corps dorms, the bunks are just bed coils which hold the mattresses. Clint, a Sergebutt in C-Artillery, liked to take a running start and leap on his top bunk landing flat out, like a high jumper. His unique mode of getting into bed inspired some of his buddies to try an experiment designed to take a little of the spring out of his step.

One night, when Clint was known to be out having a few drinks, his pals replaced the springs in his bed with pieces of string. Clint returned from his evening of merriment, spied his nice soft mattress and came on the run. With two big bounds and in perfect form he hit the top bunk flat on his back, but his journey didn't stop there. The mattress snapped through the strings, dropping all the way down to the bottom bunk.

The quickly sobered Sergebutt looked up to see a dozen freshman laughing outside his window. Alas, Clint's high jump career was nipped in the bud and he was noted for his cautious approach to sleeping the rest of the year.

♦

THE SHORT-SHEETED FROG . . . All Aggies know

what it is to be short-sheeted: you take the top sheet, fold it under so that it is only half long enough and whoever gets in bed can only stretch his legs out about half-way. It usually only takes once before the victim catches on to what has happened to his bed.

This Frog transferred to A&M from Lamar University and he wasn't as quick on the uptake as other Fish were. The first night a sophomore buddy short-sheeted the frog. He jumped in bed, rustling around trying to put his feet through the sheets, unable to stretch his legs out. His roommates watched in amusement until he finally got up saying, "Hmph, what's wrong with my sheets?"

He finally fixed them, but the next night they did the same thing again. The third night he decided to hide in the closet, waiting to catch the short-sheeting culprits. When two Pissheads walked into his room, he leaped out yelling, "Ah ha, I gotcha trying to short-sheet me again!"

"Come on, Frog," they protested, "How can anybody be stupid enough to think we would short-sheet you three times in row? I mean two times is the world record."

The embarrassed Frog passed it off as just being unfamiliar with all the traditions.

On the fourth night they all went out and had a few beers, and while they were gone, you guessed it, the freshmen came in and short-sheeted him again. The Frog was feeling no pain when he got home that night, and without thinking, jumped into bed, ramming his legs right through the sheets with a mighty RIIIIIIP. Convulsed with laughter, his Pisshead buddies rolled him out of bed until he looked like he was wearing a huge diaper.

Parading him up and down the halls, the Frog's buddies finally decided he had "grown up" from missing his freshman year at A&M.

THE GREAT CHRISTMAS COVER-UP. . .

Christmas time on campus means the anticipation of going home, with everyone enjoying a little decorating to enhance the mood of holiday cheer. There was one Aggie from Notrees, Texas, who had more spirit than sense.

Years ago, at the old President's house, a few small cedar trees could be found planted around the yard. About two weeks before Christmas, under the cloak of darkness, the Aggie spotted those nice little trees, pulled out a small hatchet he happened to be carrying, and chopped one down. Back in his dorm room, he had no lights, but managed to decorate his tree with red and green paper chains and a few other miscellaneous items.

Then the word went out that a tree had been stolen from the President's yard and that the campus police were going to conduct an investigation in Dorm 5. Now, Aggie buddies sometimes can do terrible things to each other, but when it comes time to rally around and support each other, they are equally as good at that. The word came that the dorm was going to be searched that night at 7 p.m., so the Aggies had to work quickly.

Heading out toward Tunis on back roads, the Aggies found a big pasture of cedar trees. Working like madmen, they cut down 75 trees, all about the same size as the one that was taken from the President's yard.

By the time of the inspection, there were 75 trees gracing all 75 dorm rooms, standing tall and proud. No one was charged with stealing trees, and the misguided Aggie learned a valuable lesson in loyalty and the true meaning of the spirit of the holiday season.

THE UNWANTED WATER BED . . . One way or another, a senior in the Corp of Cadets is guaranteed to be tricked, abused, or surprised by the Fish in his outfit. It just goes with the territory.

One senior was so proud of his leadership position that he had freshmen doing everything for him, from carrying his chow to cleaning his room. The senior went home one weekend and, of course, the freshmen who stayed behind were all so lonesome for the senior, they decided to do him a really nice favor.

It seems that the senior had been complaining about not being able to sleep well in his hard bed. So, the sympathetic Fish contrived a way to help out. Heading down to the community shower, they placed a board over the drain, and after sealing up some of the windows, they turned the showers on. When there were about two feet of water, they went and fetched the senior's bed and submerged it in the shower room. Water covered the bed and mattress by a good three inches.

When the senior returned that night, he went roaring down the hall, rightly suspecting the Fish of purloining his bed.

"Freshmen, come here!"

Out in the hall they came, ball-headed and grinning, the picture of inno-cence.

"Where is my bed?" demanded the senior.

"Well sir, you were complaining about the bed not being comfortable, so a group of us decided to chip in and get you a water bed. Come on and we'll show you."

Sure enough, there it was, a bed in the water. One unlucky Fish spent the next few nights on the floor until the senior's bed dried out. Even though they all agreed the plan had been all wet, they didn't think for a minute that their efforts had gone down the drain.

MOLASSES COOKIES FROM HOME . . . There
was once a good Aggie named Fritz from down in Schulenburg, Texas, who would always bring back a big oatmeal box full of molasses cookies made by his mother. Now, Aggies are generally known for their love of homemade cookies, but not these particular sugar bombs; they tasted like sweet car lube.

Fritz would bring these things back, gather all the guys in his room and offer them a cookie. One taste was enough.

"Where did you get these cookies?" asked his buddy, Wendell.

"My mamma made them," Fritz replied.

With that, the guys who had been about to throw them in the trash or spit them out had to gulp the horrible things down.

The next time Fritz went home, sure enough he returned bearing another full box of the molasses marvels, and again he called all his good buddies into his room.

Knowing what was coming, they tried excusing themselves, but Fritz insisted. Not wanting to hurt his feelings, reluctantly they gathered around. The thought of having to choke down another round of molasses cookies was almost more than they could bear.

Just in the nick of time, Wendell, their silver-tongued savior, came to the rescue.

"Fritz, we sure love your mamma's cookies, but don't you dare open that box," intoned Wendell. "These guys are just a bunch of scavengers. Save those for yourself; we can't appreciate those cookies like you do. Now you just close that box and, for heaven's sake, don't hand us any more of those cookies. It's just not fair to your mamma or to you."

A rather puzzled Fritz replied, "Well, okay," as he closed the box on those nauseous nuggets.

Wendell was elevated to hero status for sparing his pals that day and later went to use his diplomatic prowess as mayor of a town in South Texas.

OLD TRIPOD . . . Aggies are confirmed dog lovers, and no dog needed more love than the pitiful-looking creature that was always running around in front of the MSC a few years back. Yellow and mangy-looking were the dog's best features; he also had only three legs. Nonetheless, the Aggies all fell in love with the bedraggled mutt and appropriately named it Tripod.

Over a four-year period, ol' Tripod must have slept in at least 300 different rooms. It was just another tradition and considered part of your responsibility to make sure that Tripod had a warm place to sleep and plenty to eat every night of the year.

One night, a junior transfer student who didn't know about the Tripod tradition returned to his room to discover the unlovely animal asleep in his bunk. He became enraged that a dog would be in his bed. Just as he started to grab the dog, two other guys in the room grabbed the junior and said, "No no, you can sleep on my bed, but don't mess with Tripod. That is his bed for tonight."

When Tripod died, a crowd of fifty Aggies attended the funeral of their canine buddy.

PHYSICS STUDENT FINDS GRAVITY . . . Several years ago, almost all the major classes in liberal arts were held in the Academic Building. With no air conditioning, it sometimes didn't matter how exciting the professor or topic might be, students just couldn't help but fall asleep in class.

One day, Chris, from Lufkin, Texas, was sweating through an English class on the second floor about half asleep. There was a history class being held on the floor above her where the professor let people sit wherever they wanted. Jake, a physics major from Brownfield, Texas, opted to sit on the window sill to catch the breezes.

Meanwhile, Chris, on the floor below, just happened to be looking out of the window in time to see a body fly by, falling from the third floor of the Academic Building, fast asleep. It seems that Jake had succumbed to the heat and the law of gravity. Chris couldn't believe what she had seen. Running over to the window, she saw Jake hit in a clump of shrubs right next to the language department. He was awake and groaning a little bit, but alive.

To this day, people don't know how he survived the third-floor fall, except that between the prof's lecture and the heat, he was so relaxed and sound asleep when he hit the ground, he was able to escape serious injury.

It was obviously the case of the physics major who fell hard for history.

THE FISH SMELL . . . One very cold fall, a sophomore from Plano in one of the Air Force squadrons became the victim of the worst the chemistry lab had to offer.

It seems that this particular Pisshead had far exceeded the bounds of approved behavior and was due for some kind of humbling reminder from those who suffered under his insane ravings. Everyone in the Corps at the time knew about Bab-O bombs and the severe penalties for employing this type of retaliation. The memories were still fresh of what had happened to the Fish from the outfit downstairs who had set off the last Bab-O bomb. So the Fish in the offending Pisshead's outfit decided to forget about explosives and launch a chemical warfare assault instead.

Being new to the mysteries of A&M's chemistry department, some of the more enterprising Fish decided to apply their new-found knowledge of organic chemistry to this offending upperclassman. They reasoned that the most foul smell emanating from the human body was that of vomit, and they had recently learned that the source of this odor was butyric acid. Off to the lab they went and, sure enough, bottles of this repulsive chemical were available to someone who didn't have the purest of motives.

After much debate on the best method to launch their chemical weapon, the Fish determined that a 50-cc syringe filled with a concentrated solution of butyric acid and fitted with a very long needle could be used to contaminate the Pisshead's room without ever going inside it (Fish not having the infamous pass-keys available to juniors). The coldest stretch of winter weather was deemed the correct time to strike.

The result has gone down as one of the most putrid examples of revenge in Corps history. The disgusted sophomore, and his semi-innocent roommate, were unable to enter their room for almost two weeks, and then only after the door and window had been left open 24 hours a day for the entire period.

To this day, those of us who were there can vividly recall the nauseating stench of the ultimate weapon. Some three years later, a group of copy-cat raiders applied a weaker solution to the interior of a wing commander's senior boots. He still wore them, but no one got any nearer than they absolutely had to.

The Bab-O bomb Fish is now a prominent businessman in Houston; the offensive Pisshead from Plano ultimately became outfit C.O. and is now reported to be a practicing physician. The wing C.O. with the wretched boots was last seen in the Officer's Club bar in Osan, Korea, complaining about the U.S. Air Force and his career.

COMPLEX VARIABLES . . . Graduate students at Texas

A&M manage to have a little fun in spite of the seriousness of their tasks. A trio of buddies who were all working on Ph.D.'s in educational administration were notorious for the tricks they pulled on one another. One of the group, Johnny, was an absolute illiterate in mathematics and the chief prankster. His buddies, Norvell and John, finally decided to get even.

It seems that Johnny was about three-quarters of the way through his Ph.D. program, lacking only his dissertation. John and Norvell knew one of the secretaries in the math department and enlisted her help in the prank. They arranged for her to call Johnny, telling him that he had to take Math 666, Complex Variables, if he was going to complete his doctorate and graduate from Texas A&M. According to the secretary, no one was allowed to graduate until he had taken Complex Variables.

The tricksters had arranged for the secretary to call Johnny while they were all together. Johnny came unglued.

"You can't believe what that woman told me," he moaned. "I am going over there right now and tell her I don't have to do that."

"Do what?" they asked innocently

"Take a graduate math class," said Johnny.

"Well, we had to take it," they assured him. "Everybody has to take it. If you want to graduate from Texas A&M, you have to take Complex Variables."

Johnny was really upset about the proposed change in his degree plan. He ran up the stairs of the Academic Building to the math department on the third floor, unaware that his two buddies were sneaking along behind him.

"What is this about me having to take Complex Variables?" Johnny demanded as he walked into the math department.

Calmly, the secretary said, "Yes, you have to take it to graduate. Do you want to talk to the Department Head about it?" About that time, the two buddies sidled into the office and leaned against the wall.

When Johnny turned to look at them, his horrified expression proved to be too much, and the culprits dissolved in laughter. Johnny uttered a few words that wouldn't pass in polite company while his buddies and the secretary enjoyed a laugh at his expense. Lunging at his tormentors, the trio made quite a spectacle dashing around the third floor rotunda with one of the group hollering, "I'm going to kill you if I can catch you! I am going to kill you if I can catch you!"

All three of them eventually got Ph.D.'s and went on to become successful scholars and educators. Sometimes, you wonder how.

WORKING CLOTHES . . .

A student had an appointment with the dean of the College of Agriculture, a man who was an absolutely beloved individual and highly respected. Thousands of students had been helped by this kind, scholarly gentleman.

The Aggie had been working out in the pasture with the livestock, and you can imagine what he looked like in his old boots with dung on them, old jeans and shirt. He lost track of time and didn't have time to clean up before his appointment with the dean. Running over to the Agriculture Building, he was sitting in the waiting room when the dean walked out. To his surprise, the dean said, "Come on, son, follow me."

The student didn't ask any questions; he just got up and followed the dean. They went downstairs where, at the dean's request, the Aggie loaded some cattle and feed and fixed a couple of trailers. Some two hours later, the young man turned to the dean and said, "Sir, you don't understand. I didn't come here to work; I came here to have an appointment with you at 2 o'clock." The dean replied, "Bill, I know that, but let me tell you something. The next time you come for an appointment with the dean, you dress accordingly. When I saw you sitting there, I figured that, with the way you were dressed, you had come to load trailers and do the kind of work you have just done. Am I right or wrong?"

Well, I can assure you that the next time that young man had an appointment with that dean, he was dressed with a coat and tie. Clothes may not make the man, but they sometimes make the man's work.

THE GENETICS GENIUS . . .

One of the favorite professors on campus during the Sixties and Seventies taught genetics. Having taught the same course for many years, he had his timing, problems and answers down pat, even to the hour and minute of each class.

Two Air Force senior cadets, William and Tom, always sat on the front row so as to not miss any of the professor's entertaining lecture. Although it was a large class and the questions were few, both cadets loved to be prepared and able to answer when called upon.

One fine spring day, Tom was listening intently to the particulars of today's genetics problem. No one remembers whether this was one of the famous banty hen problems or the dreaded roan cow problems. Suffice it to say that Tom was just sure he had the right answer when the prof began, "Now, class..."

This phrase was the clue that he was looking for a volunteer to offer the number of offspring from the question that had been posed. Up jumped the eager cadet and shouted out, "Four, Sir!"

"Wrong!" shouted back the professor, appalled that one of his best students could shove his foot so far down his wide open mouth.

Tom shrank down low in his chair as the professor continued with the lesson. Suddenly, there was total silence.

"Now, class," began the prof again, "I must apologize. Stand up, Tom, and face the class. I have taught this class for many years and on this, the 15th class period, I have always given the same problem. I've never changed this problem until today, and I now discover that I have made a grave error.

"Tom gave the correct answer. I had transposed a number that I have never messed up in the past. Mr. Mendel, you may be excused and take the rest of the period off!"

Head held high and boots flashing, Tom strutted out of the room and departed for the MSC. The genetics whiz is now a practicing dentist in Austin with quite a few offspring of his own to keep track of.

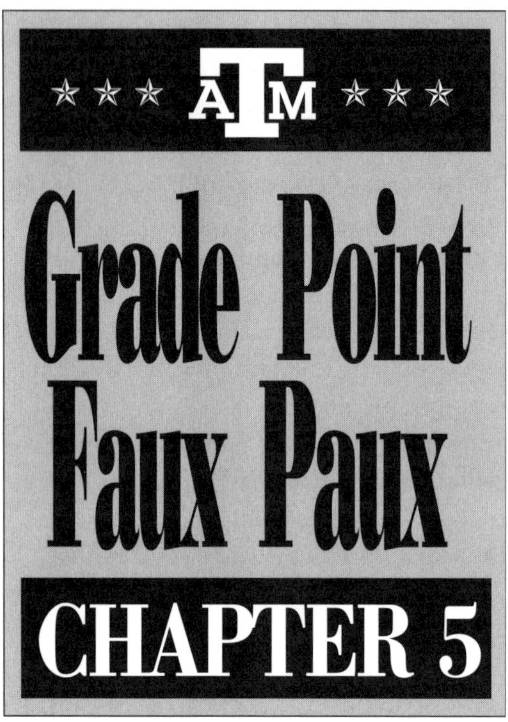

An Ace in the Classroom . . . Someone is always trying to beat the system, and while no one likes to admit there is academic dishonesty, sometimes you have to admire the creative techniques.

In this particular instance, there was a final examination in chemistry being given, and an unprepared football player sat down behind a well-prepared tennis player. The skinny little tennis player was known to be a straight-A student; the same, however, could not be said for the reserve linebacker. Not that he was a bad student, but with all the practicing, he was just too worn out to study.

Knowing how important it was to pass the test, the big linebacker was determined to peer over Jake's shoulder for the answers. Finally, he whispered, "Write darker, dammit." Everybody around him kind of chuckled. Finally, he said it again, a little bit louder, "Write darker, dammit, and move over so I can see."

Little Jake whispered back, "I know the answers, but I can't let you see them." The next thing the rest of the class saw was a big meaty hand reaching out to grab a handfull of flesh on Jake's back. The football player pulled so hard, Jake's eyes were squinted. After that, Jake moved over to the side of his seat, but wrote down some wrong answers, which the linebacker promptly copied.

As it turned out, the linebacker flunked the exam, but the tennis player served an ace.

THE BUNGLED REACH. . . Back in the Bear Bryant days there was a player on the team who had a gambler's streak in him — he wasn't lacking in the intelligence to pass his classes; he would just rather take a risk than study. The time arrived for a very difficult biology examination. The player was unprepared, so he started asking around trying to locate an old exam or, better yet, a copy of the new one.

Having heard that the professor lived in a boarding house in College Station, the football player sought advice from another student who had already had the same class. Sure enough, the student supplied him with everything he needed to know.

"He lives in a boarding house and goes home for lunch every day," said the student. "He carries his briefcase with him to his room on the bottom floor, then goes in the back room to eat lunch."

The day before the big examination, the football player enlisted the help of a friend to drive to the professor's boarding house around noontime. Sure enough, the scouting report had paid off; the professor arrived, briefcase in hand. After watching him walk into the house, the brazen football player marched up to the door and knocked. The little old lady who ran the house answered, and the jock asked if the professor was home. "Oh, yes," she assured him, "he is here, but he is eating lunch right now."

"I won't disturb him," said the football player, turning to leave. As soon as the lady was out of sight, he did an about face, opened the front door and ducked off to the professor's room. Snagging the briefcase, he reached in, found a copy of the examination and ran back to the car.

His pals in the car scribbled the questions just as fast as they could, and then the daring jock turned right back around and returned the purloined exam to the prof's briefcase.

Alas, the football player's double daring dash failed to pay off. The next day's examination was totally different because the football player had stolen and copied the wrong test.

He and twelve of his classmates failed to profit from his "boarding house reach."

THE WINDED WATCHMAN . . . One thing that is always passed down from year to year is the location of old quiz files. Some professors are notorious for giving the same exams every semester, year after year. So when preparing for big tests, it's common practice for Aggies to head for the various quiz files at the Corps, sororities, and fraternities. Occasionally though, a band of midnight riders will go one step farther in their quest for good grades.

In this particular case, a group of young men decided to plan an assault on the Agriculture Department. They had a really tough exam coming and were willing to risk it all to pass. Among the perpetrators was a big guy named Louie. Weighing in at about 220 pounds and a towering 6'2", Louie was elected the group's lookout.

After casing the building, the group decided to try digging through the trash inside, especially by the secretary's desk, in hopes of locating the stencil that had been used to run off the exam. This was before the days of computers, which have made tests more secure.

When the group went into the building, Louie decided to station himself in a nearby tree to keep watch. In case of campus police, Louie would give a two-whistle warning to his buddies. Well, Louie went scampering up that tree as fast as his 220 pounds could carry him, crouching on a limb some twenty feet off the ground.

Just as he was about to get settled in his perch, the campus police turned into the parking lot, heading right for Louie's hideout. With the threat of exposure, Louie got a little excited. Not only would his whistle not work, but his foot slipped off a limb and he came crashing down through the tree. Louie hit the ground with a mighty THUD that knocked the wind right out of him.

Desperate to warn his compadres, Louie tried in vain to muster a whistle. "Heeez" was all he could manage; he couldn't catch his breath. "Heeez," came the sound again, from under the bushes where he had rolled.

Inside, one of the gang happened to hear Louie's desperate wheezing and saw the campus police coming. The group ran off, leaving poor Louie gasping in agony under the brush. Somehow, Louie managed to curb his wheezing and hide until the police went on by.

There was no test stolen that night, but one "watchman" was skinned up and bruised for a long time, serving as a reminder that, when you try to beat the system, sometimes the system beats back.

AN ATHLETE'S ACADEMIC FALL . . . Bear Bryant

had some exceptionally talented athletes during his tenure, and one player, Don, was an exceptional pass receiver, punt returner, and defensive back. He was also something of a dare-devil. He was so good that Coach Bryant did not allow him to take part in contact drills or scrimmages because of the fear he might be injured before a big game.

That season, the TCU Horned Frogs came to town sporting an undefeated record. During the course of the game, Don intercepted three passes, caught one touchdown and virtually single-handedly beat the TCU Horned Frogs, putting the Aggies in first place in the Southwest Conference. During the game, it was obvious that no one could even get close to this elusive player. He came out of the game almost unscathed in that glorious victory.

Monday morning, one of Don's buddies noticed that he was limping.

"Don, I didn't see you get hit in the TCU game. Why are you limping?"

Don replied, "You're right, I never got hit. Nobody touched me. But, Sunday night after the game, I got to worrying about a quiz that was coming up on Monday.

"I was up on the ledge of the second floor of the Academic Building trying to sneak into the prof's office to find the quiz. Just as I climbed in the window, the prof walked in and turned on the light. It scared me so bad I fell into the shrubs below and twisted my ankle when I hit the ground.

"Remind me never to climb around on that ledge again. Next time, I'll just study."

Fortunately, Coach Bryant never found out that his championship season hopes had been dangling off the second floor of the Academic Building.

A LESSON IN SOCIOLOGY . . . The old Sociology Building was the site of some tough exams. One night, a football player named Billy decided the only way he was going to score on the next day's exam was if he first touched down in the professor's office and located a copy of the test. Enlisting the help of his buddy Richard, from Hico, Texas, the two snuck into the building only to discover that all the offices were locked up tight.

Not ones to be discouraged, Billy noticed a small window over the top of the office door.

"I can get through there," he confidently assured Richard.

Making sure the coast was clear, the 220-pounder stepped on the door knob, hoisted himself up and started through the transom window. About half-way through he discovered he was wedged tight. Unable to move front or back, Billy panicked and began calling to Richard to for help.

By now, Richard was a little panicked himself. Running to the other end of the hall, he dragged a huge table over to the door, making an awful racket. Standing on the table, he tried in vain to pull his buddy out, but he wouldn't budge. Not knowing what else to do, Richard grabbed Billy's feet and pushed him on through the window.

There was one awful crunch when that football player hit the floor. He tried to get out, but the door had a deadbolt and wouldn't unlock from the inside. With both boys in a state of near apoplexy, Billy seized the moment, grabbed an office chair and smashed through the big plate glass window in the door, all thoughts of looking for the exam wiped from his mind. Heedless of the glass fragments, he scrambled through the hole and the two would-be thieves escaped into the night.

When the students showed up for class the next morning, the shattered window was taped over with a large sign reading, "Boys, stay out of my office and quit trying to steal my examinations. I don't keep them in here and you are wasting your time." (Signed) Prof Dan.

STERLING BUTTERFLY . . . Sterling C. Evans Library is an attractive building with lots of glass to allow plenty of light to enhance the study environment. One night, there were a number of students down in the reference room preparing research papers. It was just before dark when Mary, a graduate student, looked up and noticed a strange figure running from Frances Hall right toward the library.

This was not your average looking student. This particular individual was in the buff, completely covered with a heavy coat of shaving cream, running wide open toward the library window. The students inside stood up and started talking about what was going on. The human shaving bomb hit the big window like a bug on a car windshield. Waving his arms and legs, he made a huge butterfly figure on the window, much to the amusement and consternation of the students and library staff.

After he had made his impression, he smiled, turned and sprinted off toward Scote's Hall, just him and the remnants of his shaving cream.

Mary turned to another student and said, "Well, that is probably the only time he ever exposed himself to books."

THE DUPLICATING PARKING PASS . . . Parking on campus has become a real nightmare these last few years, with heavy competition for spaces that are less than two miles from your classroom. A few years ago, one of the perks of being in a student leader position like Battalion editor was being issued a staff parking sticker with a number one overlay. In traffic-lingo, it meant you had been handed an unlimited license to park—any lot, any time, anywhere.

Understandably, these stickers were highly valued and closely guarded, with only a relatively few being issued each semester. One such lucky recipient was generous enough to occasionally lend the sticker to a few close friends with the understanding it would be promptly returned.

However, one pal borrowed it so frequently that the student leader was forced to drop a few subtle hints that the lending days were nearing an end. Surprisingly, the pal returned the sticker a few days later, saying he wouldn't be needing to borrow it again.

Now, the student leader was a trusting sort and never bothered to ask why the close circle of pals suddenly no longer required the loan of the parking pass. Not until after graduation did the truth come out.

It seems that one of the pals was a really talented photographer and very creative in the darkroom. He also had a part-time job at a local printing company. Rather than keep pestering his friend for the parking pass, he decided to make a copy of his own. Several days of experimentation paid off, and a duplicate was achieved that was shear perfection. Even the director of campus police would have been hard pressed to identify it as a fake. Being an obliging fellow, the forger cranked out a few more copies for his closest friends. All of them, that is, except for the holder of the original permit.

Fortunately, all involved graduated before campus police bothered to compare serial numbers on the growing numbers of cars that appeared on campus sporting staff permits with number one overlays.

*T*HE *G*REAT *D*R. *P*EPPER *R*AID . . . In the late Fifties each dorm had two drink machines—Coke and Dr. Pepper proudly stood side by side. Each would serve a drink and ice in a paper cup for a mere ten cents.

The trouble was that the Dr. Pepper machine often would omit the ice and the unlucky Aggie would have to drink his soda warm. Or, sometimes you got cup and ice, but no Dr. Pepper. The most infuriating was when the machine would deliver ice and Dr. Pepper — but no cup. All you could do was watch your drink, and ten cents, pour down the drain.

At the end of "Call to Quarters" study period each night, it was the custom of the sophomores in "A Chemical Company" to gather at the Dorm 3 machines and sample the wares. After one long frustrating week of defective beverages, the group decided to send the Dr. Pepper Company a not-so-subtle message about the chronic defects in their machines.

The word went out and by morning's light, all twelve machines were piled high, bonfire style, in the center of the quadrangle. A sign in large letters was placed atop the stack admonishing: "You have stolen your last dime!"

Dr. Pepper was not amused. The company pulled all their machines from across the campus. Thus, for more than thirty years, Dr. Pepper machines have not honored Texas A&M by their dorm presence. It brings a whole new meaning to the slogan, "Be a pepper..."

*T*HE *S*TUD OF *A*LL *S*TUDS . . . Mother Nature is not known for being evenhanded when it comes to passing out good looks, and there was one junior who had really gotten a raw deal. Pimply and chubby were his best attributes, and his buddies always gave him a hard time because he didn't have a girlfriend.

The other fellows would meet these beautiful woman on Corps trips, often bringing them back to campus for visits. But nobody of the fairer sex ever came to see poor ol' Elmer. What his buddies didn't know about Elmer was that he had a sister who was absolutely beautiful. She later went on to become a movie star and was a 10 in every measure.

One day, Elmer and all his buddies were at the MSC having a cup of coffee. As usual, the fellows were all bragging about their beautiful dates — all except Elmer, of course. About that time, in walks Elmer's gorgeous sister. She strolled by four or five of his buddies, shaking her head, saying, "No you're not my type. I want somebody who is strong, handsome and has all the qualities I am looking for in a man."

Turning to Elmer, she winked, gave him a big hug and kiss and said, "Come home with me, dream man." They walked out together, Elmer with his chest thrown out and head held high, the most beautiful girl on campus on his arm.

Elmer never did reveal the secret identity of his "best girl," and from then until he graduated, his new nickname was "The Stud of all Studs."

Incidentally, Elmer did get married to a very charming young woman, and they now live in Weslaco, Texas, with their three children. Maybe the scene with his sister gave him confidence, after all.

THE BIRTHDAY MOONING . . . A relatively recent

chapter in the history of Texas A&M University has been the recognition of sororities and fraternities. They have become a viable part of the University, attracting outstanding students and doing a lot of good projects to improve the community. They have also added a few good stories to pass down.

There was a young sophomore from Dallas who pledged the Sigma Chi fraternity. His girlfriend went to SMU, so naturally he made frequent trips back and forth to Big D. He was also known to date on-campus occasionally, as long as his girlfriend at SMU didn't find out.

Parent's weekend was coming up, and it just so happened to coincide with this young man's birthday. But as luck would have it, no sooner had his parents called to say they couldn't come because they were going out of town, than the poor fellow's Dallas girlfriend also called to cancel out. She wished him a happy birthday by phone, leaving him with only his fraternity brothers to console him.

The weekend came and Saturday afternoon, with nothing better to do, the young man went out jogging. Sweaty and weary, he stopped off at a friend's room to shoot the breeze, then decided to take a shower before returning to his own room. After the shower, he wrapped his T-shirt around his waist and headed down the hall to his room.

He jerked the T-shirt off just as he opened the door. Flipping on the light, he was welcomed by the chorus of "Happy Birthday" from his girlfriend, his parents and fraternity brothers. Only the surprise turned out to be on his unexpected visitors, since the birthday boy was wearing nothing more than his birthday suit.

THE BONFIRE BUNGLE . . . Back in the Fifties, the bonfire
was built on the drill field in front of the Memorial Student Center. Aggie outfits took turns guarding the bonfire while it was being built. The weapons were logs and army socks filled with big bars of soap. If you have ever been hit upside the head with an army sock with a bar of soap in it, you know you'll be down for about two weeks.

One afternoon about 5:30, the numbers of guards were few, and there was generally not much activity going on around campus. I witnessed this, and I'll tell it like I saw it.

A 1955 Chevrolet Bellaire came roaring down in front of the YMCA building, down past the Coke Building, past Goodwin and Bizzell, and, making a quick right, came to a stop near where the review stand sits. Out jumps a guy with a can of gasoline who runs toward the bonfire, splitting the ranks between two freshman and throws the gasoline on the bonfire. He tears off toward the Grove while another fellow jumps out of the Bellaire and comes running toward the bonfire. He flips a match at the bonfire and it goes up with a WHOOOOSH, followed by nothing more than a small fizzle of smoke.

Well, Aggies all know that you don't light the bonfire with a bucket of gasoline and a match, but these tea sippers or similar low-lifes didn't have that kind of sense.

The Bellaire roared on around toward the Grove to rendezvous with the strike force. The door opened and the guy who had thrown the gasoline jumped in the back seat. The guy with the matches had two freshmen in hot pursuit, and one of them had already gotten in a good lick with the soap sock so the ol' boy was a little dazed. He was running wide open and, just as he got to the getaway car, the wind blew the door shut. The fellow dived into the door and was knocked about half out. The freshman caught up with him and grabbed him just as the car stopped to assist the fallen buddy. The Aggies beat the car mercilessly with logs, breaking windows and making dents, but the would-be arsonists still managed to retrieve their compadre and drive away.

As far as I know, that is one of the few attempts ever made to prematurely light the greatest traditions of them all, the Texas Aggie Bonfire.

THE FIRST FREEZE . . . Some traditions at A&M disappear because the "scene of the crime" disappears in the face of construction and campus expansion. Henderson Hall used to be home to the athletes and directly behind Henderson was a pool that has since been covered over. An outdoor swimming pool in the Brazos Valley can be used all but about four months out of the year, but a few devious upperclassmen felt it was their duty to make sure the pool got at least one use during the winter months. Starting along in November, the upperclassmen began warning the Fish to get ready for the first freeze. The naive freshmen hadn't a clue what lay in store, but were understandably curious after the big build-up.

It was the middle of January when the first hard freeze hit Aggieland, and a thin glaze of ice covered the pool — truly a glorious sight. Not wanting the Fish to miss out on the view, the seniors awakened them at six in the morning and lined them up near the edge of the pool. The Fish were instructed by the seniors that they thought it was more in the spirit of things if the Fish wore nothing more than their jock strap.

Standing outside in the freezing cold, the freshmen soon began to comprehend their fate. The upperclassmen instructed them to line up behind the diving board and jump into the pool one at a time. One freshman, named Robert, decided it would be wise to go first, figuring it would be that much sooner that he was reunited with his clothing and warm dorm room.

Making his way to the front of the line, he literally had to fight for the privilege of the first jump. Robert jumped off the board, feet first and teeth clinched. Breaking through the thin layer of ice, he quickly made his way through the frigid water and, pulling his shaking body out of the water, he headed for his dorm. One of the seniors stopped him and said, "Where do you think you're going?"

"Back to my room, sir," he chattered.

The senior laughed and said, "You have to wait out here until all of your friends have jumped in."

Only after they had all taken the refreshing dive were the blue, shaking Fish dismissed. To this day, Robert remains cautious about volunteering to go first for anything, especially in the winter.

THE GROSS AGGIE . . . Not long ago, an Aggie grossed out his dinner companions in the Sbisa chow line when he decided to add an unusual pork dish to the menu. Grabbing a tray, he started down the hot food line. Reaching inside his coat, he pulled out a dissected piglet from the biology lab, all opened up where you could see the ghastly-looking parts.

Laying it on his plate, he didn't say anything; he just walked right through the line. All of the cooks serving the food turned pale, and everybody else in the line backed away from him and his haute cuisine.

"Hey, everybody, they got fresh pig today," he cajoled. "Whoooo Haaaa. Come and get some fresh piglet."

Well, I can assure you that no one pigged out on the hot food line that day.

FLAG FOOTBALL HEROES . . . In recent years, flag football has become a very competitive intramural sport, with more than 100 teams working their way through the tournament bracket hoping to become champions and receive the coveted tee-shirt. Few people realize the talent involved in flag football, with many of Texas A&M's non-football intercollegiate athletes playing on teams.

Not too long ago, there was a rag-tag team of students who had all grown up together in College Station. They had all played sports in high school, but none of them were what you would call sports legends. In fact, most of them were better known for the time they spent on the bench than their athletic prowess. Their quarterback, Johnny, had played basketball in high school and rode the pine so much that he was dubbed "Johnny Bench."

Also on this unlikely line-up was Chuck, who didn't look like any kind of an athlete at all. Chuck was maybe 5'4", if you stretched him, and he weighed about 135 pounds with his shoes full of water. However, he did have one physical feature that made him unique among flag football athletes, and that occasionally came in handy during games — Chuck only had one eye. He had a prosthesis that covered his whole eye socket, so when you met him, it was fairly noticeable that he had only one eye.

Somehow this group of misfits managed to make it to the championship game, the Super Bowl of flag football. Most attributed their winning record to being more creative than their opponents, something that would be crucial in the final game as they faced off against an opposing team whose players were all members of Texas A&M's baseball and track teams.

Chuck made it a point to have a friendly pre-game chat with the referee, making sure they noticed his false eye. As tough as Chuck was, he knew how to work the officials, knowing this bit of psychology sometimes came in handy during a tight game.

As it turned out, the match developed into a close, low-scoring game. The home-town boys found themselves down by two points going into the fourth quarter, and things did not look good. It was time for desperate measures.

One-eyed Chuck was an offensive lineman for the team, and, of course, in flag football, no contact is allowed. The linemen are not even allowed to use their hands. But it was decided that the time had come for Chuck to take a fall. As the ball was snapped, Johnny threw a short pass that fell harmlessly to the ground. It appeared to many that the local yokels' Cinderella season had ended. However, lying on the ground, writhing in fake pain, was good old Chuck. And lying next to him was a beautiful yellow referee's flag.

Chuck's teammates rushed to "help" him, drawing even more sympathy from the officials. The call was a personal foul, and it was worth ten precious yards. Chuck's Academy Award winning performance gave the natives a first down and new life. Victory followed a few plays later.

THE LAST RING DANCE LAUGH . . . The annual Senior Ring Dance is close to the hearts of all students, symbolizing the culmination of their achievements at Texas A&M. On the big night, dates are escorted through a massive ring, and the class year numbers on senior rings are turned from the inside to the outside to signify that the Aggies are now ready to graduate and go out and challenge the world.

There was a graduate student who had gone to a smaller school and probably went around telling lots of Aggie jokes — until he earned his Aggie ring. He decided to attend Ring Dance as a graduate student. An electrical engineering major, the fellow was plenty intelligent, but lacked in what are commonly called the social graces.

Even though the dance didn't start until 8 o'clock, the fellow persuaded his wife to show up two hours early so they could have their picture made while they were still "fresh."

Sure enough, they were first in line to have their picture taken inside the big ring. They then waited patiently for two hours for the dance to start.

All during the evening the fellow had big fun laughing at the people who had to wait for pictures, and he delighted in telling everyone that he and his wife had been first in line.

Two weeks later the Ring Dance pictures were sent out to everyone except the couple who had been first in line. As fate would have it, the film had been bad for the first shot.

Even though they were "fresh" for their picture, they ended up being fresh out of Ring Dance photos.

SEEING EYE REVEILLE . . . Reveille accompanied the Aggie football team to the Kick-off Classic in 1988, and it was a great opportunity for the team and the mascot to see New York City and the Statue of Liberty. But much to the disappointment of Reveille's handler, dogs are not allowed on public transportation in New York City — the pair was unceremoniously thrown off the bus.

Undaunted, the determined trainer made a fast purchase of some very dark sunglasses and a cane. After some minor adjustments to Reveille's leash, the pair successfully boarded the next bus, with much help from the driver to

accommodate the trainer's "handicap."

Seeing is believing and Reveille, and the enterprising blind trainer, got to see the Big Apple and the Statue of Liberty, after all.

TRI DELTS AND A WALTON WARRIOR . . .

Spring Break — two words guaranteed to conjure up some memories and some smiles. After a winter of studying, the onset of spring and that magical break in routine are a combination that sends students in droves to places like South Padre Island; they go looking for fun, sun and future memories.

One bunch of Aggies took off for this mecca seeking girls and good spirits. They rented a condo near the center of an anonymous-looking complex, row after row of similar-minded fun-seekers.

These Aggies hailed from Walton Hall and found themselves right next to a condo full of Aggie Tri Delts. A beach party ensued and, as the night got longer, the party got louder until, finally, about 4 a.m., the guys decided to surrender and get some rest. Back at the condo, a head count revealed that one of the Walton warriors was missing. Nobody could find him, though they looked high and low.

The one place they never thought to look was next door, amongst their Tri Delt neighbors. It seems that the missing Aggie had one too many beers, staggered into the wrong condo, and passed out on the floor. When the women came back, they didn't know who he was, but he was wearing an Aggie t-shirt, so they just covered him up and left him.

The next morning, the Aggie woke up to a headache and an eye-full. His hostesses introduced themselves and even served him breakfast. He apologized for the unexpected sleep-over and went swaggering back to his own condo full of coffee and some creative memories.

Of course, Aggies would *never* exaggerate a story, though some of the Aggie's Walton buddies did express their suspicions. Anyway, the whole episode made for quite a Spring Break memory to remember.

NO CHICKEN AT THE CHICKEN . . . The Dixie Chicken

is a legendary Northgate watering hole that all Aggies find soon after arriving in College Station. When Aggies come back for twenty-year reunions, the first thing they want to do is hit the Chicken.

As many as three to four thousand Aggies have been known to gather at Northgate along University Drive to enjoy a longneck and bask in the glow of an Aggie victory. Of course, there are those who take a little longer to get the hang of absorbing the area's local color.

It seems there was a Yankee who had just arrived to go to school at Texas A&M. Spotting the Dixie Chicken, he strolled in and went up to the counter saying, "I want some southern fried chicken."

"What do you mean, 'southern fried chicken?'" came the perplexed reply.

The Yankee looked a little funny, saying, "Well, Dixie pertains to the South and doesn't the sign say 'chicken?' I want some fried chicken."

The conversation had attracted the attention of several Chicken regulars, and the place got very quiet. After an awkward moment or two, the old boy

behind the bar who pops those longnecks handed the Yankee a Lone Star and said, "Look, buddy, you are obviously not from Texas, I understand that; and you are certainly not from College Station. We got longnecks, we got pool, we got dominoes, and we got fun. But we got no chickens here, fried or otherwise."

THE MANHEIM MASSACRE . . . Between Caldwell

and Austin is a little town called Manheim, Texas, boasting a somewhat famous old filling station where generations of Aggies have stopped to get a hunk of cheese, cold beer or Coca-Cola and to have a little conversation with the owner before continuing on their journey.

One particular night, many years ago, a group of Aggies were coming back from a t.u. game all fired up because A&M had actually won one down there. Sure enough, they stopped in Manheim. One of these enterprising Aggies saw a box of cherry bombs. You can't buy cherry bombs anymore, which is probably wise, but at the time, you could buy a whole white box full of them. The store owner sold them the cherry bombs, wondering the whole time why they were buying them. The Aggies drove about a half mile up the road and saw twelve mail boxes in a row. Now, why an Aggie would even think about this, I don't know, but one of them mused, "I wonder what these cherry bombs would do to a mailbox?"

The thought was like itching powder on the already revved up group, so they stopped. There were four Aggies and twelve mailboxes so each Aggie was issued three of the highly explosive cherry bombs. A wager was placed to see how many bombs they could light and close up in the boxes before they exploded.

Four of them lined up, opened the mailboxes, lit all twelve cherry bombs and started throwing them in the mailboxes. By the time the first box was blowing up, the fuses were burning in the others. The Aggies jumped in the car and, looking back, saw that all twelve of the mail boxes were gone.

They roared off toward Caldwell, thinking they had made a clean getaway, but pretty soon along came the highway patrol. Apparently, the farmers along the road had heard the explosion, saw the mailboxes gone and called the police. The Aggies were apprehended in Caldwell.

The officer brought the befuddled culprits back to face the farmers. The Aggies bought the mailboxes, apologized and went on back to campus without any further punishment.

A few years ago, a professor and a student who had heard about the story were going through Manheim and decided to stop. There was the owner, a little grayer, but the same man who had been there 30 years before. Quietly, the professor directed the student to ask the gentleman if he had any cherry bombs.

"Sir, do you by any chance have any cherry bombs?" the young man asked.

The little grey-headed man said, "You get outta here, boy. My neighbors haven't spoken to me for over 30 years since a bunch of Aggies with cherry bombs blew up their mailboxes."

The graduate student got a big kick out of his reaction and the professor laughed knowingly.

THE BOLSHOI BLUES . . .

Given the choice between a ballet and a barbeque, a lot of Aggies would choose the latter. Jeans and a t-shirt are the preferred dress code for most students. But in an effort to bring more refined entertainment to Aggieland, the MSC Opera and Performing Arts Society was formed and began recruiting such suit and tie occasions as symphonies and plays to campus.

After an ardent effort by OPAS to attract a big-name program to Aggieland, their endeavor was rewarded with the announcement that the world-renowned Bolshoi Ballet had elected to hold its world premier of *The Nutcracker* in the Rudder Auditorium. Perhaps in the spirit of warming relations between the two world powers, the artistic director of the ballet extended an invitation for A&M officials to attend an invitation-only presentation of *The Nutcracker* in Moscow. One of the OPAS student representatives, who hailed from College Station, was selected to go.

Like most Aggies, his clothing of choice for class was well- worn jeans and a t-shirt. And, being a serious student, the Aggie made a point to attend all of his morning classes before making his dash for the airport to catch his plane East. He arrived at the airport just in time to check his luggage and grab his boarding pass. His new tuxedo safely checked through to Moscow, Derek sat back, relaxed and enjoyed the flight.

As dependable as most airlines are, it has been known to happen that, from time to time, luggage checked at one end doesn't always make it through to its intended destination at the other end. And, as Fate would have it, there was no luggage on hand when he landed. Unable to buy any clothes, and the performance only two short hours away, Derek was forced to improvise. His head held high like a true Texan and Aggie, he attended the Bolshoi anyway, in blue jeans, cowboy boots, t-shirt and a borrowed bow-tie.

B Q Entrepreneurs & George Bush . . . The

Aggie band was invited to George Bush's inaugural festivities in Washington, D.C., in 1988. When the Aggies got up there, they were quartered in Maryland some 20 miles from D.C. Having no funds to get everyone around town to see all the sights, two of the more enterprising members of the group hit on the idea of renting transportation. Unfortunately, all the cars in the area were rented, so David, Class of '91, and his "ol' lady" hit on the genius idea of renting a U-Haul truck to go sightseeing. Figured carefully, it would cost each member of the group only about $2 per day. They loaded about 35 guys in the back of the truck with four in the front seat who paid a premium of $5 for the privilege. The

van was parked in the back of the motel to prevent the band director, Col. Haney, from discovering their unusual mode of transportation.

When the U-Haul truck arrived in Georgetown the first evening, the back doors swung open, and 35 skin heads poured out to the amusement and consternation of the Georgetown sophisticates. Only four of them at a time got to sight-see, but the others agreed that at least it was a cheap way to get around Washington, D.C.

David's father was surprised when his credit card statement showed gasoline purchases for a U-Haul truck and, since the two Aggie entrepreneurs had negotiated to charge an additional five dollars apiece for sight-seeing in a truck with no windows, Dave and his ol' lady came home with more money than they took.

George and Barbara Bush loved the Aggie band, but if they had realized how resourceful they were, George might have kept them around to work on the budget deficit.

SHILOH DANCE HALL FIGHT... The Shiloh Steakhouse on Texas Avenue hasn't always been a restaurant. Back in the Forties, Fifties and early Sixties, it was the Shiloh Dance Hall. Lots of country and western two-stepping went on there Friday and Saturday nights. Country folks would come into town to have parties. It wasn't air conditioned, but there were some big windows, which were considered premium seating by the partiers, and you could hear the music all across the countryside.

It was considered a given that there were going to be a few scuffles on big dance nights, since the Aggies always wanted to dance with all the country gals. One evening, one little football player was really taking advantage of the situation, dancing with every woman there and having a big time. One of the farm boys took offense, walked up to him and said, "Boy, you want me to whip your tail?"

The football player replied, "No, sir, I will ask for what I want." With that, the farm boy threw the football player out an open window, and from then on it was fist city, football players against the farmers. A few chairs and tables were broken, but nobody was seriously hurt.

To this day, the Aggies that were there blame the little football player for starting the ruckus, although he swears that he only said politely, "No sir, I will ask for what I want." However, that was the last time football players were allowed in the Shiloh Dance Hall.

POPCORN, ZOOK? . . . The Campus Theater remains a Northgate landmark even though movies are no longer shown there. For years it represented the only entertainment available to Aggies for miles.

Back in the Fifties, there was a farm boy who came to A&M named Zook. A towering 6'2", and weighing in around 260 pounds, Zook had hands the size of baseball mitts. Having been a hard working farm boy all of his life, he was as strong as a bull and played a pretty good game of football, too.

Zook liked everybody and thought everybody liked him just as well. Most folks did, except for Zook's one bad habit. He would come into the Campus Theater and sit down right beside you. While you were busy trying to balance your Coke and your box of popcorn, Zook would take his big old meat hand, reach in your box of popcorn and come away with at least half of it in one swipe. He would then proceed to shove it all into his mouth at once. But he was always nice about it, saying, "Thanks."

After a while, his buddies had their fill of Zook swiping all the popcorn. Joe, an animal science major from Dallas, was taking a meat science class that semester and hit on a plan to curb Zook's popcorn manners.

That Saturday night, a big movie was showing at the Campus. Joe went in and sat down, like always, with his big box of popcorn. Zook came shuffling up, took the seat beside Joe, preparing to make his famous popcorn snatch. Just as he reached over into Joe's box, he opened with a string of curse words and hollering. It seems there was no popcorn in the box, only a three-day old cow's tongue. Zook certainly gave Joe a tongue lashing about the trick, but it was nothing compared to the one Joe had arranged to hand Zook.

THE HAT TRICK . . . It's always been a sort of standing rule that, if a professor is ten minutes late to class, the Aggies get a walk. Students scrupulously watch the clocks and when ten minutes have passed, the more courageous, or less scholarly anyway, get up and leave.

A few years ago, a group of Aggies came through and they were real clock-watchers. Eight minutes, nine minutes, ten minutes and no prof in the class, and they were out of there. What they had failed to see was a hat up on the front desk, just an old hat.

When they returned to class two days later, the prof was there — and so was the hat.

"Men and women, students, let me tell you something," intoned the prof. "When you come in this classroom and see my hat, don't leave; it means I am here."

"Yes, sir," they all dutifully replied.

Two days later, the prof walked in, putting his hat down on the desk and looking out over the 60 seats; there were 60 caps sitting on the chairs. The prof was angry at first, but then burst into laughter. The hat was on the other head now, so to speak, and he knew his trick had backfired.

THE BORING LECTURE . . . There are a lot of fine professors at Texas A&M, but occasionally there are those teachers who are less stimulating than others. A professor, whose nickname was Sandman, was droning on, waxing and waning about some aspect of animal reproduction. He looked back in the second row and there was a cowboy, head laid back, mouth wide open, snoring to bring the cows home.

The prof did his best to ignore the unconscious student, but finally, exasperated, he couldn't take it any longer. He turned to a young man on the front row and said, "Patrick, Jerry behind you there is fast asleep. Turn around and wake him up."

Without hesitation, Patrick responded, "Sir, you put him to sleep, you wake him up."

PROFESSOR FLOWER . . . At one time there was a course called Botany 101, and the professors faced quite a challenge getting the Aggies fired up about the study of plants. There was one professor who was a bit

strange anyway, but he tried his intellectual best to interest his pupils in plants of all kinds.

It was early spring and all across the Brazos Valley the wildflowers were in full bloom, inspiring the professor to try again with his lethargic students. The Texas bluebonnet is indigenous to the area, and nowhere are they more plentiful than in the Brazos Valley. So Professor "Flower" came to class with a handful of bluebonnets, raving about their beauty.

"Wouldn't ya'll like to study these?" he implored.

The reply from the class was "Hissssssss." It seemed as though the prof had failed again.

According to the story, the students were in the hot biology building, waiting for another boring lecture about plants, when the prof entered, wearing a cotton gingham dress and a big blue bonnet. He came dancing into the classroom, grasping a big handmade bluebonnet flower in one hand and a cluster of the real things in the other.

He curtsied down the rows, handing each amazed student a bluebonnet.

"Now, boys, I want you to look carefully at these bluebonnets," he chirpped. "Then I want you to draw a little dress and cut it out."

The professor then handed everyone a toothpick and some scotch tape.

"Tape the toothpick to the little dress, take your bluebonnet and put in on top of the toothpick and it will look just like a pretty little girl and just like me!"

After the Aggies got their laughter under control, they realized they had unwittingly enjoyed a rather unique lesson on the shape of the bluebonnet flower. For the rest of the semester, even though he was a little strange, the students warmed to this professor who would go to such lengths to dress up his lectures.

RAUCOUS ROD . . . Zany professors come and go at Texas A&M, but any who passed through the halls of the chemistry building during the reign of Raucous Rod will recall a professor who could teach chemistry like nobody else. Often times, a student's first introduction to the creative chemist would be when he marched into the first lecture wearing a football helmet and shoulder pads yelling, "Block and tackle for chemistry."

Just when you thought class might be settling into a routine, Rod could be counted on to unsettle things. One day, as students were fidgeting in their seats waiting for the professor to arrive, from the back of the class comes a war whoop. Pounding toward the podium comes Raucous Rod, clad in full baseball uniform and cap. As he neared the front of class, Rod dived to the floor, proclaiming, "Slide for chemistry!"

Not only was he flamboyant and funny, Rod will be remembered as a skilled teacher who knew how to have fun. Rod left A&M and went on to fame and fortune in the private sector, earning patents on unique products including a revolutionary flea "comb" for pets.

PINKY DOWNS . . . Back in the Forties, Fifties and Sixties, there was a legendary figure on this campus named P.L. "Pinky" Downs. After successful runs as businessman, community leader and member of the Board of Regents, Pinky stayed on campus and came to be known as "The Official Greeter" for Texas A&M.

It's easier to become a legend if you're the least bit eccentric or colorful, and Pinky did his part to help the tradition along. Every place he went you would see Pinky in a felt hat and a long grey top coat, walking along with a big smile on his face and his thumb in the air, saying, "Gig'em Aggies, Gig'em Aggies, Whooo Haaa, Gig'em Aggies."

He would greet anyone who came on campus, be it a visiting dignitary or some lost freshman from Bedias. You could count on Pinky Downs always to be there with a warm smile, a friendly handshake and the willingness to help. Pinky truly loved Texas A&M and the student body mirrored his affection; the 1955 *Aggieland* yearbook is dedicated to him. Pinky was a kind soul, kind to everybody, not just Aggies. Legend has it that one day Pinky heard about a drifter who had died and, in the absence of family or loved ones, the county was going to see to the burial of this unfortunate soul. A friend to all in the here and hereafter, Pinky decided to go to the funeral out of respect.

Venturing out to a small country cemetery near the edge of the county, Pinky arrived just in time for the service. One of only three people — the other two were the grave diggers — Pinky listened as the preacher made his customary remarks. In closing he said, "Before we lay this poor soul to rest, is there anybody who would like to say anything good about him?"

After a moment of silence, Pinky Downs, standing in the back with his hat in his hand said, "Yes, Mr. Preacher, I would like to say something. I don't known anything about this poor old soul, but I would like to say two or three good words about Texas A&M — Gig'em Aggies!"

Don't Mess Around With Pinky . . .

Though Pinky Downs was a permanent fixture around Texas A&M for more than 30 years, sometimes it took awhile for new students to come to appreciate his unique presence.

Pinky symbolized the spirit of Aggieland. I can see him now, in battered hat and long top coat, shuffling along, yelling, "Whooo Haaa. Gig'em Aggies." He

Pinky Downs

would regularly patrol the MSC and walk by the coffee shop, calling, "Whoo Haa, Gig'em Aggies. Good Aggies, Good Aggies."

Before every baseball, football, basketball game or track meet, Pinky would give a pep talk to the players. When he retired on the Texas A&M campus, the Aggies became his family, and he was known as the spiritual leader of Texas A&M University.

One time, as Pinky was making his ritual tour through the MSC, a non-reg spotted him for the first time. Not being in the Corps, the student was unfamiliar with Pinky Downs and, therefore, was a bit unprepared for his somewhat unique presence. He jumped up yelling, "Somebody get that old so-and-so out of here!"

Before he could finish, someone threw a poncho over the non- reg, put a couple of knots on his head and dragged him out in the hall. The lecture he got was short and to the point: "Don't you ever say anything negative about Pinky Downs."

THE SIGNING OF AN ALL-AMERICAN . . .

Stories about great athletes have a way of being enlarged through the years, so that the players who long ago left the locker room still manage to add 10 points to their batting average every year or continue to score more winning touchdowns as the years go by. One legend that Aggies love to tell is about the way a certain All-American fullback and linebacker was recruited to Texas A&M.

At the time he was "discovered," this future All-American had played only six-man football. Unknown in the college spotlights, the local folks in his hometown knew him to be a big, tall, strong young man with a lot of character and great desire to compete.

The story goes that this strong young man was out behind the mules plowing his fields in San Angelo when he was approached by a stranger. It seems that a coach on the Texas A&M recruiting staff had become lost on the backroads while trying to find a high school. Not knowing which way to go, the coach spotted the country boy across the field, plowing the straightest row you ever saw. Getting out of his car, the coach walked up to the young man and said, "Son, I'm lost. Which way is it to San Angelo?"

Without hesitation, the young athlete picked up the enormous plow with one hand, used it to point north and said, "San Angelo is that way, sir." Replacing the plow in the furrow, he called, "Good luck," and continued down the row.

With that, the coach said, "Hold it, young man, what is your name?"

"Jack, sir," he replied.

The coach said, "I have a scholarship right here in my pocket that I want you to sign. We want you to play football for Texas A&M University."

The Aggies know the rest of that story. Jack Pardee went on to become a consensus All-American, a great National Football League star, and is currently a prominent coach in the NFL. Legends and athletes, they go together at Texas A&M.

THE MILITARY WASH-OUT . . . One year during military weekend, a big banquet was hosted at Duncan Dining Hall for visiting dignitaries. President Earl Rudder, Col. Joe Davis, and members of the student affairs division were seated together at the head table when a campus policeman came in and informed President Rudder that there was a huge water fight going on out in the quadrangle.

Col. Joe, President Rudder, and the student life leader excused themselves from the banquet and stepped outside Duncan Hall. Hearing the commotion, they began walking toward Dorm Seven. Just as they rounded the corner, two CTs unloaded on them with buckets of dirty, muddy water. You can imagine

the sight of the colonel's military dress uniform and the suits worn by the other two gentleman after the liquid assault; they were soaked from head to toe.

Now, here was a great president, a great military leader, and an important university leader standing, dripping wet, in front of two freshmen who were quaking in their wet, muddy skivvies.

President Rudder looked thoughtfully at the two boys and said, "Go study, men, and break it up."

The quadrangle was cleared in record time. The gentlemen all went and changed and returned to the banquet as if nothing had happened. The visiting dignitaries had a fine time and were said to be very impressed with the maturity and exemplary behavior of the Corps of Cadets — at least the ones they saw inside Duncan Hall.

SENIORS, LONGNECKS & OLD ARMY LOU

. . . Every year in March, the Corps makes its famed March to the Brazos to benefit the March of Dimes. Each outfit solicits sponsors to raise funds for this worthy cause — somewhere between $20,000 and $50,000 are raised every year.

This is a major event in the life of a cadet because the seniors are in command as they lead the more than 2,000 members of the Corps on a seven-mile hike to the Brazos River. Once they reach the Brazos, the seniors are "dead" and the junior leadership takes over the march back to campus. By tradition, the seniors are allowed to make other, non-biped arrangements for getting back to campus and the traditional post-march celebration at the Dixie Chicken.

Over the past few years, the numbers of cars out at the river have been a hazard, so the military leaders decided to have buses deliver the seniors to the Dixie Chicken. The first year of the buses went fairly smoothly, with just one little hitch. It seems that the first bus took off with a few seniors a little early, taking them straight to the Dixie Chicken. These guys had worked up quite a thirst and managed to consume not only their rations, but also the longnecks that had been reserved for seniors who were coming on the second bus. When the second group finally arrived, they rushed into the Chicken only to discover that their beer had been hijacked. A few heated words were exchanged, tempers flared and trouble was not far away.

Fortunately, a few tables away sat Ol' Army Lou, down from Loupot's bookstore, enjoying some refreshment of his own. Understanding about Aggies, especially thirsty Aggies, Lou stepped in and offered, "The longnecks are on me. Ya'll deserve it."

Some say an army marches on its feet, but Ol' Lou knew that sometimes it marches on its promised longnecks, too.

LUKE, THE COKE MAN . . . A gentleman named Luke

has earned legendary status around campus as the well-known face behind the concession stands at football, basketball and baseball games. Luke and his wife, Polly, have been selling cold drinks, hot dogs and other goodies to grateful fans for more than forty years at Texas A&M. His smile and friendly handshake are his trademarks, and he can recall generations of athletes by name, position and their more memorable exploits. Luke has employed a lot of needy Aggies to sell Cokes over the years, some under unlikely employment conditions.

Back in the late Forties and early Fifties, the Aggies had a great basketball team with stars like Wally Moon, John Dewitt and Walt Davis. Since old Deware Field House was too small to hold the entire student body, the alphabet was used to determine who could go to the basketball games. Students whose names started with A through G could attend one night, with H through N seeing the next game, and so on. As soon as the gym was full, the doors were locked.

One night, the Aggies were taking on t.u., and some fifteen upset Aggies were left on the wrong side of the locked door. From his perch behind the concession stand, Luke was moved by the plight of the poor Aggies. Making an impromptu hiring decision, Luke instructed the lads to grab trays of Cokes or bags of ice and follow him.

The boys got in, the Cokes got sold, and Luke was forever remembered as the basketball savior.

PRESIDENT RUDDER'S STAND . . . Back in the late Sixties and early Seventies, there were numerous rebellions on college campuses around the country in the aftermath of the Vietnam War. Some universities were actually shut down by student riots and destruction on the campuses. Even though Cornell and the University of Texas had problems, very little protest took place on the campus of Texas A&M University. Word came to Texas A&M that a group called SDS was planning to march on the Texas A&M campus, their purpose being to rally the students into a riot. When the news was brought to President Rudder, he was said to declare, "That will never happen on my campus."

The leadership of the Corps of Cadets was unanimous in their decision to support President Rudder. The consensus was that, regardless of individual feelings about the war, Aggies fought and died in it, and an anti-war protest would not be allowed on campus.

The plan for the protestors was to march onto campus from Texas Avenue, right up the steps of the Systems Building and into the heart of campus before circling the President's office. Just as the march started, the protest leader was confronted by President Earl Rudder.

"Where are you going, son?" Rudder enquired.

"We are going onto campus," he replied. "That is our right."

"If you do," countered Rudder, "you'll have to go through one pot-bellied president first!"

With that, the leader of the protest group was snatched by some members of the Corps of Cadets and other students who had been backing up President Rudder's stand. Legend has it that the protest leader was hauled off campus, doused with honey, sprinkled with feathers, and run out of town on a rail.

In future years, some say the Texas legislature sure looked kindly on Texas A&M because of the incident, increasing funding because school officials were able to prevent destruction and rebellions at a time when other universities were being laid to waste by misguided students.